SHARKS

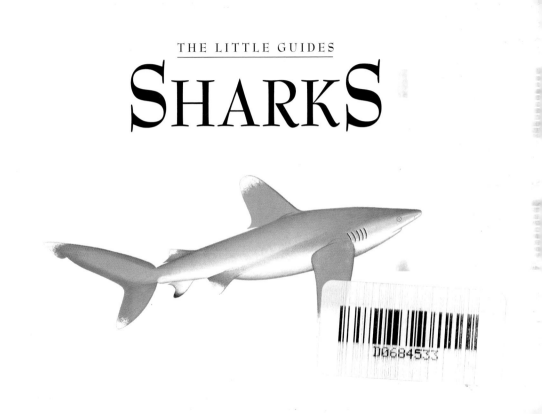

D0684533

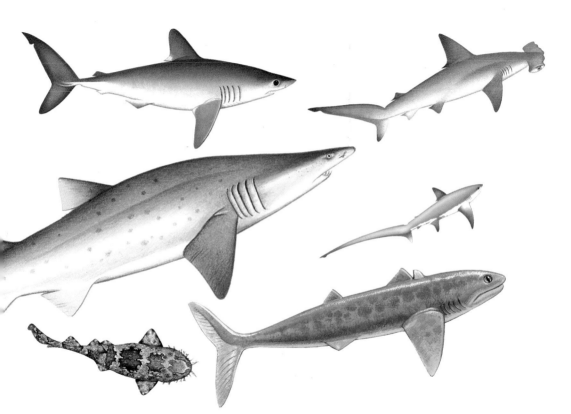

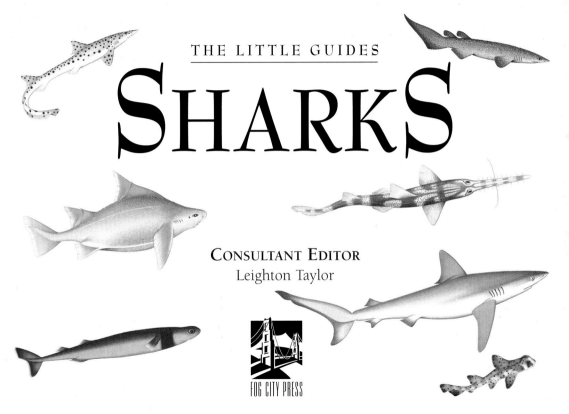

THE LITTLE GUIDES

SHARKS

CONSULTANT EDITOR
Leighton Taylor

FOG CITY PRESS

Published by Fog City Press
814 Montgomery Street
San Francisco, CA 94133 USA
Reprinted in 2000 (three times), 2001, 2002

Chief Executive Officer: John Owen
President: Terry Newell
Publisher: Lynn Humphries
Managing Editor: Janine Flew
Art Director: Kylie Mulquin
Editorial Coordinator: Tracey Gibson
Production Manager: Martha Malic-Chavez
Business Manager: Emily Jahn
Vice President International Sales: Stuart Laurence
European Sales Director: Vanessa Mori

Project Editor: Robert Coupe
Designer: Lucy Bal
Consultant Editor: Dr. Leighton Taylor

A catalog record for this book is available from the
Library of Congress, Washington, DC.

ISBN 1 875137 64 5

Color reproduction by Colourscan Co Pte Ltd
Printed by Leefung-Asco Printers
Printed in China

A Weldon Owen Production

CONTENTS

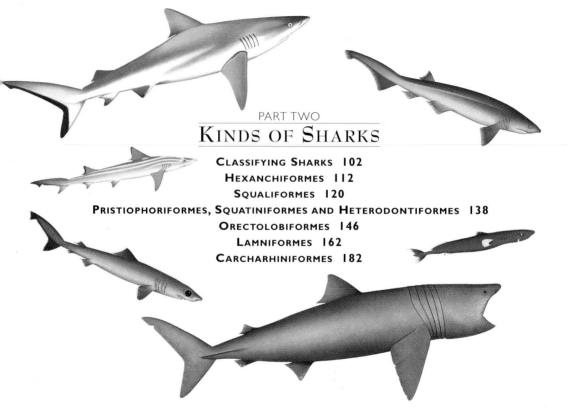

PART TWO

KINDS OF SHARKS

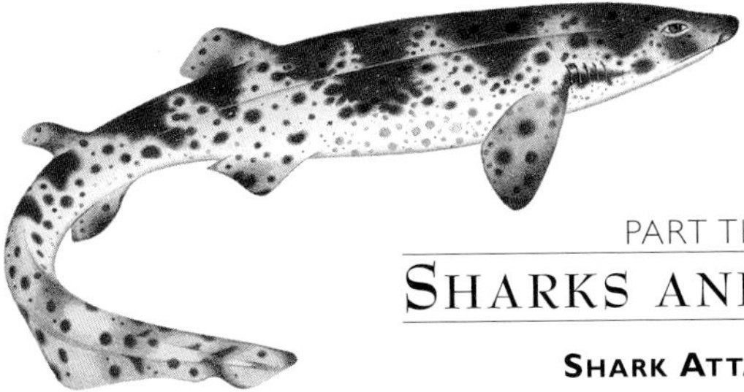

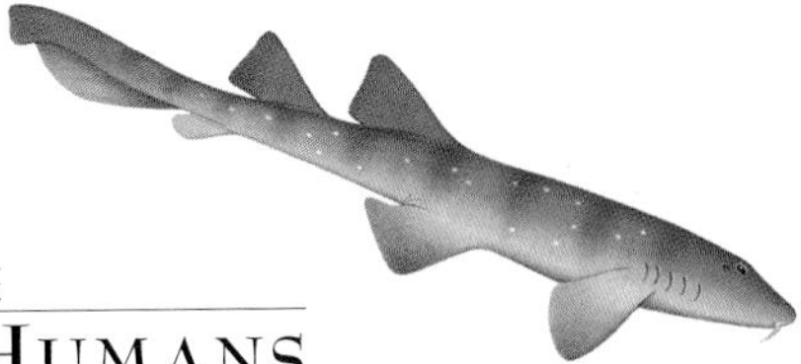

PART THREE

Sharks and Humans

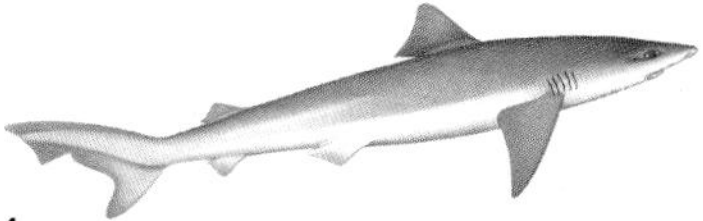

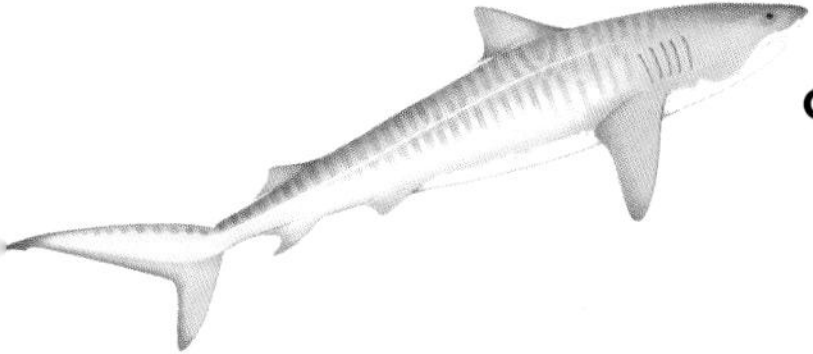

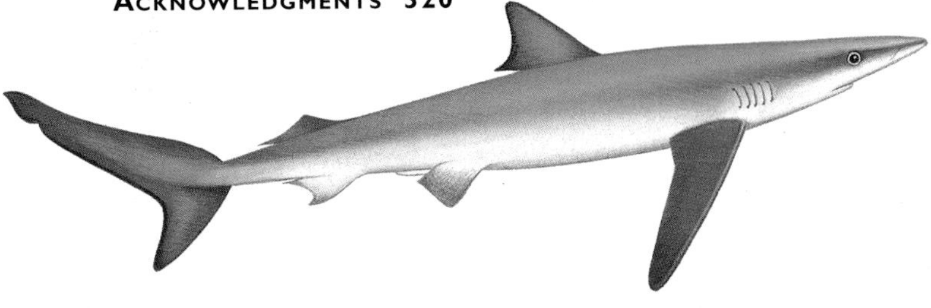

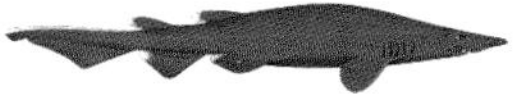

PART ONE

THE SHARK

UNDERSTANDING SHARKS

Sharks comprise only about 1 percent of all living fishes, and share most of their features with their finned relatives. Like all fishes, sharks use gills to extract oxygen from the water in which they live. They swim by undulating the tail, which creates forward propulsion. The internal anatomy of sharks and fishes is very similar. But there are a number of characteristics that separate the elasmobranchs—sharks and rays—from the other fishes. It is these unique adaptations that have enabled sharks to survive in their watery habitat.

WHAT IS A SHARK?

Sharks, which comprise only about 1 percent of all living fishes, are highly evolved representatives of a large and unique group of fishes—the cartilaginous fishes, or class Chondrichthyes (a term that combines the Greek words for cartilage and fish). Cartilaginous fishes have a long evolutionary history; they diverged nearly 500 million years ago from the bony fishes (class Osteichthyes).

OUTSIDE THE MOLD
When people think of sharks, most imagine a large, aggressive great white or mako, with fearsome teeth and gaping jaws, cutting through the water like a torpedo. While a number of sharks conform to this pattern, many do not. This Port Jackson shark, for example, is a sedentary species, and is harmless unless handled.

Characterizing sharks Sharks are jawed fishes. Like all fishes they are aquatic, water-breathing vertebrates with a brain and spinal cord; fins; plate-like pairs of internal gills; and paired sense organs. Unlike most bony fishes, sharks do not have swim bladders or lungs. Sharks' jaws are simple but effective structures, armed with transverse rows of hard teeth that are replaced slowly but continuously. These teeth are not in sockets, but attached to the jaws by soft tissue.

Fins All sharks have paired fins—pectoral and pelvic—on the underside of the body. The pectoral, or breast, fins are located just behind the gill region of the head. The pelvic fins are on the rear of the abdomen just in front of the tail. In male sharks, each pelvic fin has a clasper, or copulatory organ, for implanting

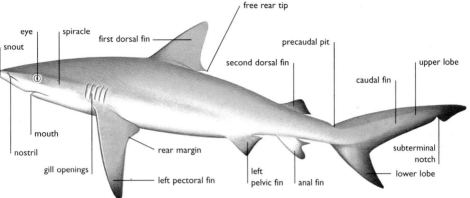

eye

spiracle

snout

first dorsal fin

free rear tip

precaudal pit

second dorsal fin

upper lobe

caudal fin

mouth

nostril

rear margin

subterminal notch

lower lobe

gill openings

left pectoral fin

left pelvic fin

anal fin

sperm inside the vent (the common reproductive and excretory opening) of the female. The vent is located between the pelvic fins in both sexes. Most sharks have a cylindrical or slightly depressed head and body; a strong tail with a caudal, or tail, fin; one or two dorsal fins on their back; and an anal fin on the underside of the tail behind the vent.

The skeleton The skeletons of cartilaginous fishes are composed of cartilage instead of bone, similar to the material found in the human nose and ears. The prominent scales, bones of the head and bony fin rays of bony fishes are absent in sharks. Instead, their bodies are covered with small, tooth-like scales, often referred to as denticles.

EXTERNAL FEATURES

This Caribbean reef shark exhibits all the common external features of sharks. While there is great diversity in shape and size between different species—and while some unusual species do not conform to popular notions of shark appearance— most features shown in this diagram appear, though often with significant modifications, in all sharks. Anal fins, for example, are not present in many species.

15

SHARKS AND OTHER FISHES

Several features separate the elasmobranchs from other fishes. Externally, all the shark's five to seven gill slits are visible, while the gills of most other fishes are protected by a bony plate known as a gill cover, or operculum. The shark's fins are thick and stiff, and lack the delicate spines that are found in the fins of most bony fishes. The shark's skin has a layer of tiny dermal denticles, as opposed to the much larger flattened scales in most other fishes.

Skeletal differences Sharks are representatives of a unique group—the cartilaginous fishes. Internally, the shark's body is supported by a cartilaginous skeletal frame, complete with a protective cartilage skull, while most other fishes have a hard, more dense skeleton made of true bone. Sharks do not have an internal swim bladder to help achieve neutral buoyancy but instead rely upon their low-density cartilage, liver oils and hydrodynamic planing to prevent them from sinking.

Distinctive jaws Some of the most notable differences in the anatomy of sharks and most bony fishes are found in the construction of the jaw, the method of its suspension from the head and the organization of the teeth. The upper jaw of the shark bears a full set of teeth, and is derived directly from the palato-quadrate cartilages that form during development from the upper mandibular arch. In the more recently derived bony fishes, this structure also supports the upper

jaw, but the major tooth-bearing elements develop from special bones derived from the skin. Similarly, the lower jaw in sharks, known as Meckel's cartilage, is formed from the lower portion of the mandibular arch during development and also bears a full set of teeth in the adult. This structure is greatly reduced in bony fishes, and forms the joint in the corner of the jaw. The teeth develop from other specialized dermal bones. In most living sharks and rays, the upper jaw is seated on the underside of the skull where it is loosely attached by ligaments and connective tissue. It is suspended from the skull by the hyoid cartilage, which attaches near the back corner of the jaw. This arrangement permits the upper jaw to be thrust out from the skull during feeding, and this is an important means by which many sharks are able to take large,

powerful bites from their relatively
large prey.

A WIDE RANGES OF FISHES

There are some 30,000 species of fishes.
No other kind of vertebrate has nearly
that many. The possession of fins in adults
immediately differentiates fishes from
other vertebrates. Fishes have succeeded
in occupying and exploiting every kind of
watery habitat, from the ocean depths to
wetlands. They vary in size from tiny gobies
less than half an inch (1 cm) to the whale

shark, which can grow to 46 feet (14 m).
Sharks differ most obviously from other
fishes in their multiple gill slits and their
outstretched set of pectoral fins, used as
hydroplanes rather than oars.

MYTH AND REALITY

The more we know, the better equipped we are to deal with sharks rationally and responsibly. Reliable information is reaching more people through books, films, magazines and aquariums, but myths still abound. Some represent the conflict between good and evil, with the shark always embodying evil. Others have recent origins in our modern folkways. The reality is much more varied and intriguing.

Misconceptions While sensational accounts make exciting reading, we can recognize them as exaggerations. More insidious effects on our thinking are rooted in another kind of myth—those of misconception. These once appeared widely in older books, but even now we can find such statements as: "the shark is a swimming nose;" "sharks are color-blind;" "the shark is a living fossil;" "sharks have a rigid upper jaw and must turn on their backs to bite." Although some of these misconceptions have a basis in fact, they are at best misleading, and at

COMMERCIALLY IMPORTANT
A newly born tope shark. The tope shark—sometimes called the soupfin or school shark—is one of the most commercially important species of sharks and is widely distributed in both hemispheres. Its flesh, fins and liver are much sought after.

SAWSHARK
With its long, saw-like snout and slender body, the sawshark belies the traditional image of a shark. Like most sharks, it is harmless unless provoked.

worst completely wrong. "The shark is a swimming nose" implies that all sharks rely principally on their sense of smell. It is true that all sharks that have been studied have well-developed olfactory organs in their paired nostrils, the size and location of which vary with the species. But sharks use a variety of sensory systems to find prey and to survive in their world.

Misleading labels The statement that sharks are living fossils implies that all species are of ancient lineage.

While it is true that there are 400 million years of fossil record through which shark lineages can be traced, only a few living types extend well back into the geological record. One example is the bullhead, or hornshark, family Heterodontidae. Hornsharks are now common along the temperate coasts of Japan, southern California, the Galapagos Islands, South Africa and Australia. The fossil record of this family extends back 160 million years to the lithographic limestone of the Jurassic Period. To give a perspective, this is the same fossil stratum in which the early ancestor of birds, Archaeopteryx, was found. Thus the bullhead family has remained relatively unchanged (at least in its skeletal structure) for the same period in which birds have undergone substantial changes. By comparison more highly evolved sharks, such as great whites, sand tigers, and makos, are believed to date only to the Eocene, about

50 million years ago, the same as many coral reef fishes. Today's scientists are helping to dispel myths and replace them with fact.

THE SHARK OF MYTH
Peter Benchley's novel *Jaws*, and the films that followed, created a mythology about great white sharks. To many people, the great white is the archetypal fearsome shark; in fact, it is a superb predator.

A DIVERSITY OF SIZE AND FORM

Sharks have an extraordinarily long evolutionary history, during which they have fine-tuned their design to suit the varied habitats in which they live. Today's living sharks are a dazzlingly diverse lot and include tiny, deep-sea dwarves; flattened, ray-like bottom-dwellers; graceful, streamlined ocean swimmers; and huge, slow-cruising filter feeders.

A rich variety Contrary to their popular image, most sharks are small and harmless to humans. Fifty percent of living species reach a maximum length of between 6 inches (15 cm) and 39 inches (1 m). Roughly 8 percent are dwarves, one of the smallest being the spined pygmy shark, which reaches 6 inches (15 cm) at maturity. More than 80 percent of sharks are smaller than adult human beings. An "average" shark might have a mature length of about 30 inches (75 cm)—hardly the monster of *Jaws* infamy. Only about 4 percent of sharks are gigantic—13 to more than 39 feet (4–12 m) long. These include the largest living fishes, the whale and basking sharks, which broadly overlap the larger whales in size. Male sharks tend to be somewhat smaller than females of the same species, although a number of catsharks reverse this.

GRAY REEF SHARK
Like other members of its family, the requiem sharks, or Carcharhinidae, the gray reef shark has a stocky body. It grows to a maximum length of 8 feet (2.5 m), but rarely exceeds 6 feet (1.8 m).

Variations in shape While the typical shark is streamlined and and sleek, many are stout and bulky. Others, such as angelsharks and wobbegongs, are flattened and ray-like in shape.

FORM AND SIZE

Sharks vary greatly in size and shape. This small selection of shark species, drawn to scale and compared with the size of a human diver, provides a glimpse of this marvelous diversity.

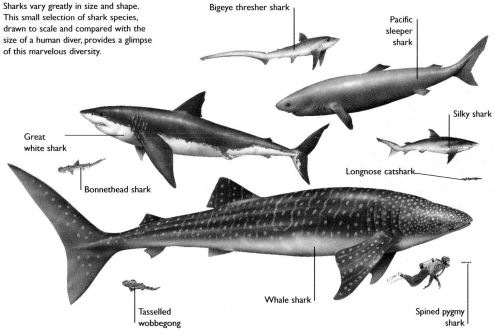

Bigeye thresher shark

Pacific sleeper shark

Silky shark

Great white shark

Longnose catshark

Bonnethead shark

Whale shark

Tasselled wobbegong

Spined pygmy shark

21

EVOLUTION

Sharks have inhabited the ocean for more than 400 million years, yet the sharks of today still look much like their ancient ancestors. Their origins, and those of other types of cartilaginous fishes, are shrouded in mystery.

AN ANCIENT MONSTER
Carcharodon megalodon evolved during the Cenozoic and may have become extinct as recently as 13,000 years ago. This relative of the great white shark grew up to 45 feet (15 m) long. Its fossilized teeth are routinely found.

The fossil record One reason for uncertainty is that for most of their history sharks have left an incomplete fossil record. A shark's cartilaginous skeleton is too soft to fossilize readily so whole fossil sharks are extremely rare. However, the hard parts, such as teeth and fin spines, fossilize easily and there is a rich fossil record of these. The first fossil shark teeth occur at the start of the Devonian, about 409 million years ago. By the end of this period, some 363 million years ago, sharks were relatively common in the fossil record. The first whole-bodied shark fossils occur during the middle Devonian (the Age of Fishes), about 380 million years ago.

The earliest sharks The evolution of cartilaginous fishes can be divided into three stages of expansion, or adaptive radiation, that were punctuated by major extinctions. The first, Paleozoic, stage began with an increase in the diversity of cartilaginous fishes in the Devonian period and culminated in the Carboniferous, between 360 and 290 million years ago. By this time, cartilaginous fishes had differentiated into the holocephalans (chimaeras) and elasmobranchs, and were the dominant fishes in marine waters. The elasmobranchs included archaic, but already specialized, early sharks, and the first of the "true sharks," including hybodonts, xenacanths and even a few modern sharks (neoselachians). This golden age of cartilaginous fishes ended as the

THE SHAPE OF SUCCESS

Long before the dinosaurs ruled the world, sharks had evolved their basic powerful, streamlined body shape. Little modification to this successful adaptation has occurred since the Devonian Period, about 400 million years ago.

Paleozoic closed about 240 million years ago with a massive worldwide extinction of species. Very few sharks and chimaeras survived, but some of the survivors became the precursors of today's sharks, rays and chimaeras.

Toward modern sharks The second, Mesozoic, stage took place between 180 and 65 million years ago. This saw the extinction of the archaic sharks, the great adaptive radiation of the modern sharks and the derivation of rays from sharks. This stage ended with another catastrophic series of extinctions at the close of the Cretaceous, about 65 million years ago. Many vertebrates disappeared entirely, while sharks, rays and chimaeras

The long-extinct Cladoselache is thought to have been a swift and powerful predator.

The tiny spined pygmy shark shares many features of ancestral sharks.

The whale shark, the largest living species, exhibits a similar body form.

were diminished in diversity. The third stage occurred during the Cenozoic, from 65 million years ago to the present. This saw the evolution of all modern sharks, rays and chimaeras.

RELATIVES: RAYS AND CHIMAERAS

Sharks and rays are members of the taxonomic class known as Chondrichthyes. They are separated from most other living fishes by having a cartilaginous skeleton. Also within the same class are the chimaeras, sometimes referred to as ratfishes, which are the closest living relatives of sharks and rays.

The blunt-nose chimaera or spotted ratfish

The ocellate river ray

What is a ray? The 600 or so living species of rays, or batoids, are essentially "flat sharks" or "winged sharks." Essentially, rays are sharks that during their evolution expanded their pectoral fins for underwater "flight" and in the process supplemented or replace entirely their tails and caudal fins. Rays are a diverse group. Some, at less than 4 inches (10 cm) long at maturity, are among the smallest cartilaginous fishes, while the manta, with a maximum "wingspan" of more than 18 feet (6 m), is one of the largest.

SHARK RELATIVES

Rays, or batoids, are the sharks' closest relatives, while chimaeras are more distantly related to sharks. All rays and chimaeras have cartilaginous skeletons without bone, and mouths and nostrils on the underside of the head.

Distinctive features Rays are similar to sharks in basic body plan, but have modifications related to their specialized form and their largely bottom-dwelling life. Their pectoral fins are enlarged and fused onto the sides over the gill openings, which are on the underside of the head. These pectoral fins are flexible, mobile, propulsive organs, capable of flapping up and down like wings. The shoulder and hip girdles of rays are wider than those of most sharks, and unlike sharks, the shoulder girdle is fastened to the vertebral column to provide a firmer base for the expanded pectorals. In most rays the section of vertebral column between the skull and the pectoral girdle is partly or completely fused into a tube, which provides further support for the pectoral fins. The upper eyelids of rays are fused to the eyeball, while in sharks they remain free. In a few blind electric rays, the eyes are covered with skin and difficult to see.

CLASSIFYING RAYS
Rays are among the most distinctive of the cartilaginous fishes, but their classification is difficult and the subject of ongoing scientific debate.

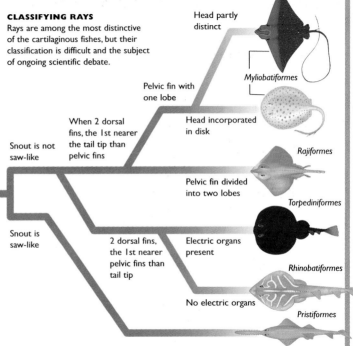

Head partly distinct

Myliobatiformes

Pelvic fin with one lobe

Head incorporated in disk

When 2 dorsal fins, the 1st nearer the tail tip than pelvic fins

Rajiformes

Snout is not saw-like

Pelvic fin divided into two lobes

Torpediniformes

Electric organs present

Snout is saw-like

2 dorsal fins, the 1st nearer pelvic fins than tail tip

Rhinobatiformes

No electric organs

Pristiformes

25

RAYS AND CHIMAERAS continued

THE PARTS OF A RAY
The illustrations at right show the distinctive features of a typical male ray. The upperside view is at far right, while the underside view is below right.

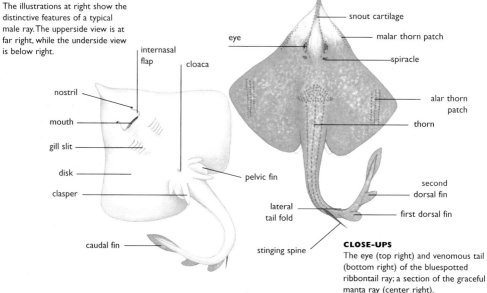

internasal flap

cloaca

nostril

mouth

gill slit

disk

clasper

pelvic fin

caudal fin

snout cartilage

eye

malar thorn patch

spiracle

alar thorn patch

thorn

second dorsal fin

lateral tail fold

first dorsal fin

stinging spine

CLOSE-UPS
The eye (top right) and venomous tail (bottom right) of the bluespotted ribbontail ray; a section of the graceful manta ray (center right).

Habitat Rays are primarily bottom-dwellers, and many bury themselves beneath sand or mud. However, some of the more advanced species, such as mantas and eagle rays, are powerful swimmers, capable of bird-like "flight" through the water and even, on occasion, the air. Rays are generally found in habitats that support sharks and are more diverse than sharks at high latitudes and in fresh water. On the other hand, there are fewer species of oceanic rays than there are oceanic sharks. The two largest ray groups—skates and stingrays—complement each other in distribution. Skates inhabit the deep slopes and inshore waters at high latitudes, while stingrays live in fresh water and in tropical regions.

Feeding Rays feed mostly on small bottom organisms and their teeth never develop into the large, scissor-like cutters that many sharks possess. However, some of the larger skates have strong jaws and pointed teeth that allow them to eat large fishes and octopuses. Some rays use their electric organs to stun large fishes and swallow them whole. Sawfishes use their snouts to stir the bottom to reveal their prey. The manta rays are plankton-feeders.

LYING BURIED
The common stingaree's flattened body is ideally adapted to burying itself in the sand. It swims off the bottom only to feed, reproduce or escape from predators. The narrow, flattened shape of a stingaree's cranium allows its flexible snout to grub for food. A stingaree's nostrils and mouth have a well-developed sensory system for locating prey.

RAYS AND CHIMAERAS continued

Reproduction Rays use two types of reproductive strategy: egg laying (oviparity) or a form of live-bearing (ovoviviparity) in which there is no placental attachment of the embryo to the mother. In all species, male rays, like sharks, fertilize females internally, using their claspers, the modified inner edges of the pelvic fin. Skates are the only rays that do not give birth to live young. They lay rectangular leathery egg cases that are anchored or attached to the bottom. Embryos may take more than six months to develop.

Live-bearers In the ovoviviparous rays, the embryos either swallow nutrients secreted from the mother's uterus (as in torpedo rays) or absorb nutrients via string-like extensions of the uterus that reach the gut through the spiracles (as in stingrays, eagle rays and butterfly rays). A newborn pup is sometimes more than 50 times as heavy as the unfertilized egg. Rays have long gestation periods and produce relatively small litters, which makes them vulnerable to population collapses from habitat degradation and overfishing.

FORM AND FUNCTION
The body shapes of rays have become highly modified and specialized. They are flattened, and the pectoral fins and body are joined to form a distinctive structure known as the "disk." Members of major families are easy to recognize but species can be confusingly similar in form. The bluespotted ribbontail ray (far left) is common in the tropical Indo-Pacific. The southern fiddler ray is one of the aptly named shovelnose rays. The plain-colored smooth stingray (above) is the largest of all stingrays and can weigh more than 770 pounds (350 kg).

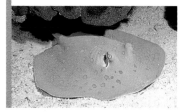

Chimaeras Termed silver sharks in Japan and ghost sharks in Australia, chimaeras are rather obscure, cartilaginous fishes. Little is known about them biologically with the exception of the elephantfishes, which support relatively large fisheries in the Southern Hemisphere. The split between elasmobranchs (sharks and rays) and holocephalans (chimaeras) occurred early in the evolution of cartilaginous fishes. Today's chimaeras are the remnants of a host of holocephalans.

Sharks and chimaeras

Chimaeras are not very shark-like in appearance, having a compressed form similar to some deepwater bottom-dwelling fishes. Shallow-water chimaeras are more silvery than sharks, but deepwater chimaeras tend to have the somber hues of deepwater sharks and rays. Unlike sharks, chimaeras have an erectile first dorsal spine and fin and three pairs of tooth plates that continually grow and wear down. These tooth plates protrude from the mouth much like rats' teeth and probably inspired the names "ratfish" and "rabbitfish" for some species. Chimaeras have a soft external gill cover with a single, rear gill opening on each side, while sharks have five to seven pairs of external gill openings. Males, like male sharks, have claspers on the pelvic fins, but they have an additional lobed clasping organ in front of each pelvic fin and another clasping organ on the forehead.

Characteristics Chimaeras are bottom-dwellers that grow to about 2 or 3 feet (60–90 cm). They never enter fresh water, nor are they active coastal or oceanic swimmers. Most of the 50 or so recognized species live in deep water on the slopes of continents and islands. This is why they are rarely observed.

LONG AND SHORT SNOUTS

Although they represent less than 5 percent of all cartilaginous fish species, chimaeras are reasonably diverse. The elephantfish (above left) is named for its unmistakable snout. The blackfin ghostshark (below) is typical of the shortnose chimaeras, or ratfishes.

THE TYPICAL SHARK

If asked to draw a typical shark most people would sketch something like the illustration of the blue shark on the page opposite. The notion of the typical shark is probably best represented by many of the requiem sharks, whose superb grace as they move efficiently through a demanding medium, 800 times as dense as air, is indisputable.

Body form The body form of sharks is related to their way of life. Our typical shark has a streamlined, slender body, a longish snout and pectoral fins, a tail fin with the upper lobe longer than the lower lobe and a thickish caudal tail stem. The forward part of the body is flattened to reduce drag during rapid turning and to allow lateral movement during normal swimming. The elevated middle sections induce more drag; they act as a fulcrum when the shark turns. These "typical" sharks swim with a slightly sinuous eel-like motion.

ACTIVE REEF-DWELLER
The silvertip shark shares many characteristics with other requiem sharks and, apart from the white tips on its fins, looks very like many of the other gray requiem sharks that are found out beyond the reef edges in warm tropical waters. It feeds on small fishes, squid and octopuses associated with the reef environments.

Silky shark

Buoyancy control In general, sharks control their position in the water by balancing opposing forces generated during forward motion. The longer upper tail lobe drives the shark down through the water, and this is counteracted by lift generated from the pectoral fins and the flattened ventral surfaces of the head region. Buoyancy control with minimal expenditure of energy is important in maintaining an animal's position in the water. One of the most important developments contributing towards this was the replacement of bone with cartilage, which provides a lighter and more elastic framework.

Skin and friction A shark's skin consists of dermal denticles, and so has a rough texture. At first sight this might seem to increase drag due to friction. It has been suggested, however, that the alignment of the denticles channels the water, resulting in a flow that acts to reduce friction. The denticles of faster pelagic sharks are smaller and lighter than those of more sluggish benthic or bottom-dwelling species.

Muscles Sharks have two main types of muscle: red and white. In the typical shark, the red muscle lies just under the skin and outside the white muscle. Red muscle functions in sustained slow swimming and in a typical shark comprises about 11 percent of the total muscle. White muscle is used only during fast sprint swimming.

TYPICAL AND ATYPICAL
The blue shark and the silky shark, with their streamlined bodies and highly efficient system of movement, typify the requiem sharks. Mackerel sharks, such as mako sharks, are conico-cylindrical and stouter of body, but are also powerful swimmers. Angelsharks, with their more flattened form, are more typical of sluggish bottom-dwellers.

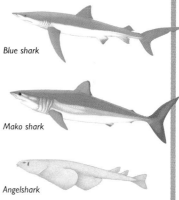

Blue shark

Mako shark

Angelshark

ADAPTATIONS: MACKEREL SHARKS

A shark's body form and locomotion are related to its way of life. Having looked at the features of a typical shark, we can now examine the ways in which species have become specialized. Over and above differences in size, about 40 percent of shark species differ significantly from the typical body plan, as represented most typically by the requiem genus *Carcharhinus*.

Thresher shark

Fast and active One family, the Lamnidae or mackerel sharks, has become highly specialized for a pelagic existence. The mako is probably the fastest and most active of all sharks and is renowned as a sportfish, often repeatedly leaping clear of the water when hooked. The body form of the mackerel sharks is conico-cylindrical, with the maximum width occurring well forward on the body. They are stouter than the typical shark and most closely conform to a perfect hydrodynamic shape. They have a bluntly pointed snout, thin caudal tail stem and a tailfin whose lobes are usually about equal in length. The tail has a high ratio of height to length, which produces maximum thrust with minimum drag and provides almost all of the propulsion.

GREAT WHITE

The great white is almost perfectly hydrodynamic. Its stiff, tuna-like body allows it to cruise for long periods at relatively low speed—until it encounters animals that it includes in its diet.

Crocodile shark

In contrast to the sinuous movement of requiem sharks, these sharks swim with a particularly rigid action.

Body temperature A major adaptation of mackerel sharks is the ability to maintain body temperatures well above ambient water temperature. This allows the muscles to operate more effectively. In a unique experiment, a 16-foot (4.6 m) white shark was tracked for several days while its depth, muscle temperature and the water temperature were recorded. It swam at an average speed of 2 miles per hour (3.2 km/h) and stayed mainly in the thermocline (the boundary between warm and cold water) where it kept its muscle temperature at 37–41° Fahrenheit (3–5°C) above ambient temperature. Mackerel sharks have larger amounts of red muscle which, unlike in other species, is sited deep in the body. The red muscle is connected to the circulatory system by a capillary network that acts as a heat exchange to reduce heat loss.

Cruising speed These sharks are well adapted for maintaining high cruising speeds and parallel many of the adaptations shown by tuna, which have a similar lifestyle among the bony fishes. Mackerel sharks' bodies tend to be denser than those of the typical sharks. The porbeagle, for example, has a density of about 3.2 percent in water and has a relatively smaller pectoral and caudal fin area. But because their cruising speed is significantly higher, mackerel sharks are able to develop sufficient lift with a heavier body and smaller fins.

Shortfin mako

ADAPTATIONS: BOTTOM-DWELLERS

In contrast to the more "typical" active pelagic and benthic sharks, characterized by streamlined bodies and a high degree of hydrodynamic efficiency, bottom-dwellers have in general become adapted to a more sluggish existence. Many of them spend most of their time on the seabed in shallow water, moving little except when they catch passing prey.

Sluggish sharks A group of sharks which are adapted to a fairly sluggish existence, and which feed on or near the bottom in shallow water, include the carpetsharks and catsharks. They are characterized by a large head, tapering body and weak, thin tail. They swim with a pronounced eel-like motion, with the motive force provided by the whole rear end of the body—and not just the tail. As they swim, the front of the body swings in a wide arc with the pivot point near the first dorsal fin, which is situated well back on the body. An important adaptation of many of these species is camouflage and many of them, including wobbegongs and angelsharks, blend with the sandy bottoms or rocky reefs which they inhabit. Some larger bottom-dwellers, such as nurse sharks and zebra sharks, are more active. These sharks, which grow to 10 to 14 feet (3–4 m) long, are reasonably strong swimmers.

The Pacific angelshark (left) and the ornate wobbegong (below) are both sluggish bottom-dwellers.

IN HIDING
Lying for the most part on the bottom of inshore rocky reefs, where it feeds on fishes and invertebrate prey, the tasselled wobbegong is protected from predators by its natural camouflage.

Buoyancy Because they spend much of their time on or near the bottom, buoyancy is not so important for bottom-dwelling sharks. Neither do they need large amounts of red muscle for continuous cruising. This is illustrated by the smallspotted catshark, which has a density of 4.7 percent and around 8 percent red muscle. Since drag is not a major consideration, these sharks tend to have larger fins that give them greater maneuverability on the bottom. Many species do, however, need to be able to accelerate rapidly to catch their prey, which they do with the help of larger, more posteriorly placed median fins, such as those of the nurse shark.

Livers and oil Some species of sharks, notably the dogfish sharks, the frilled shark and the goblin shark, have invaded the deep sea. Many of these have large livers that contain up to 90 percent oil. One of these compounds, squalene, is extracted commercially from shark livers and used as a base in the cosmetics industry. Many deep-sea sharks either have a low body density or are neutrally buoyant. Food is scarce in the deep sea and these species need to be more active than their shallow-water counterparts. Because the density of liver oil varies little with water depth, these sharks can rise quickly toward the surface after prey more easily than can bony fish, which have gas bladders for buoyancy.

ANGELSHARK
The Australian angelshark is one of 15 described species of angelsharks. These sharks have mottled dorsal surfaces and their large pectoral fins, which extend forward over the gills, contribute to their flattened ray-like appearance.

ODDITIES

The great majority of shark species do not fit neatly into the mold that is generally supposed to contain the typical shark. Most sharks, for example, are small and harmless to humans. Others look, at least to the inexperienced eye, more like rays than sharks. Still others exhibit extreme, and even bizarre, forms of body shape that have developed as adaptations to their environment and their needs.

The great hammerhead (below) and the goblin shark (right) are among the most unusual-looking shark species.

Huge plankton-eaters The two largest sharks, the whale shark and basking shark, feed on plankton by cruising slowly, filtering water through their gill slits. The basking shark has a large liver containing squalene and is close to neutral buoyancy; it can thus travel slowly, using its small pectoral fins to provide lift. The whale shark, too, is probably also close to neutral buoyancy. Generally similar in body form, despite their size, to the mackerel sharks, the basking and whale sharks are powerful swimmers, as fishers who hunt them for their liver oil can attest. In contrast, the

Left: The suction mouth and teeth of a cookiecutter shark.
Below: With its huge, gaping jaws, the megamouth shark is aptly named.

third plankton-eating shark, the recently discovered megamouth, appears to be a weak swimmer with its soft, flabby body and fins. A deep-swimming shark; its density is reduced by poor calcification, loose skin, and flabby connective tissue and muscles. This reduction of body tissues and weak swimming ability may be responses to a nutrient-poor environment.

Body shapes Extremes of body form are evidenced in, for example, the hammerheads and the frilled shark. One function of the bizarre head of hammerheads is to act as a "wing," providing extra lift at the front of the shark that enables it to bank quickly. The frilled shark is an example of extreme elongation. Its deep-sea habits are poorly known, but its long, eel-like body may be an adaptation to life on a rocky sea bottom, where this species may hunt for prey hidden in crevices. The frilled shark's jaws can be protruded so it can feed on large prey, rather as a snake does; the long body provides less resistance in the water should the shark be dragged along by its prey.

UNUSUAL FEEDING BEHAVIOR

Also known as the cigar shark, the cookiecutter shark has jaws and lips that form a suction cap on the skin of its prey. Its teeth then gouge out chunks of flesh.

SPIKY SNOUT

A sawshark is immediately distinguishable from other shark species by its saw-like snout with its distinctive pair of barbels. Sawsharks are, however, sometimes confused with sawfishes, which are rays and which do not have barbels. Sawsharks probably use their snouts to disable prey.

THE SHARK'S WORLD

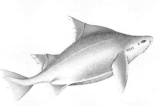

Sharks are primarily marine fishes, inhabiting a world from which humans are largely excluded. While we readily travel the surfaces of the oceans, our penetration into the watery world of sharks is imperfect and incomplete. Submarines and submersibles allow us to descend into the ocean depths, but they offer only very limited contact with sharks. Swimming and diving with sharks provide closer contact, but ultimately reinforce just how different their world is from ours. We simply do not have the variety of sensory equipment to perceive the underwater world as sharks do, and consequently it appears a profoundly alien place.

THE OCEAN HABITAT

In many ways, the ocean world of sharks is stable, predictable and forgiving. The fluctuation in daily temperature is low in most habitats, mainly because there is so much water. Mass movement is usually caused by slow, wind-driven currents or coastal upwellings, which result in relatively minor changes.

Challenges Despite the ocean's many amenable features, it also imposes some unique challenges. Water presents a very dense environment and calls for an efficient power engine and hydrodynamic design to produce rapid movements during swimming. The high salt content of the oceans constantly removes water from the soft body tissues and requires efficient water barriers and physiological mechanisms to replace it. Because of the low oxygen content of water, ingenious oxygen-extraction factories have evolved in the gills. Relatively

REEF DWELLER
The ornate wobbegong is a well-camouflaged bottom-dweller that inhabits rocky and coral reefs. Wobbegongs range from shallow waters to depths of over 330 feet (100 m). The ornate wobbegong is common around most of the Australian and Papua New Guinea coasts.

The gray reef shark is the shark most familiar to divers in deep waters of central Pacific reefs. It is particularly abundant in deep areas on the seaward side of the reef flat and also in deep areas of the backreef or lagoon.

Darker depths The deep, dark, cold regions of the ocean provide a relatively inhospitable environment, and many of the sharks that are found there make regular migrations into the higher zones. Although many species of sharks are collected at depths below 3,300 feet (1,000 m), few could survive exclusively in this region because of lack of food resources.

low visibility in the oceans has resulted in many specializations of the eye and the evolution of specialized sensory organs.

Different habitats Many habitats are recognized in the world's oceans. Coastal reefs in the higher latitudes, kelp forests along temperate coasts, coral reefs in tropical regions and sea grass beds adjacent to many reefs are some of the habitats that harbor a diversity of marine life that provides food for different species of sharks.

Inshore and farther out
Continental shelves that surround landmasses and the upper parts of the continental slopes are home to many shark species. As waters become deeper shark numbers decline markedly. In the nutrient-poor epipelagic waters far out to sea only a few species are found.

WIDE-RANGING
The great white shark's penchant for seals means that it is often seen in cool coastal waters, though its range also extends to the open ocean and to tropical areas.

WHERE SHARKS LIVE

Sharks inhabit almost every marine ecosystem on Earth and are distributed throughout all the world's oceans. They are most varied in temperate and tropical seas, in the shelf waters of continents and islands and on the adjacent deepwater slopes. There are few species in the upper reaches of the open ocean and even fewer in very deep water.

Temperate waters Temperate latitudes are usually dominated by small requiem sharks, bullhead sharks, catsharks, houndsharks, piked dogfish sharks and sometimes angelsharks. These frequent rocky reefs, muddy bottoms of bays and open sandy habitats. Larger sharks in temperate waters differ from smaller sharks by swimming constantly over large ranges. Great white sharks are seasonal visitors to temperate coastal waters near rookeries and haul-out sites for seals and sea lions. Sand tigers and many large requiem sharks frequent coastal areas adjacent to their normal ranges above continental shelves.

Tropical reefs Sharks most commonly associated with the bottoms of tropical reefs include

LOCAL AND GLOBAL
Above: The Port Jackson shark ranges around most of the coastline of Australia, including Tasmania.
Far left: The huge whale shark, the world's largest living fish, is very widely distributed in all tropical and subtropical oceans. It is often found in coastal areas.

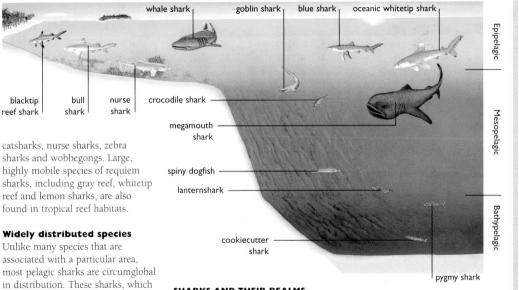

whale shark | goblin shark | blue shark | oceanic whitetip shark

Epipelagic

Mesopelagic

Bathypelagic

blacktip reef shark | bull shark | nurse shark | crocodile shark

megamouth shark

spiny dogfish

lanternshark

cookiecutter shark

pygmy shark

catsharks, nurse sharks, zebra sharks and wobbegongs. Large, highly mobile species of requiem sharks, including gray reef, whitetip reef and lemon sharks, are also found in tropical reef habitats.

Widely distributed species

Unlike many species that are associated with a particular area, most pelagic sharks are circumglobal in distribution. These sharks, which inhabit all ocean depths, include the epipelagic blue shark, the mesopelagic crocodile sharks and the bathypelagic cookiecutter.

SHARKS AND THEIR REALMS

Different ocean realms are favored by various species of sharks for a variety of reasons, including the availability of food and individual adaptations to particular environments. As well as types of localities—coastal, reef or open ocean— three distinct depth levels are identified in the above diagram.

ACTIVE TROPICAL SHARKS

When classified according to water temperature, sharks can be divided into three groups: tropical, temperate and cold-water sharks. Sharks abound in marine waters of the coastal tropics. Moving away from the coast, species are less diverse, though there are more epipelagic species in the tropics than in colder waters.

Tropical species Tropical sharks live in areas where the water temperature is usually warmer than 70° Fahrenheit (21°C). These sharks include most of the requiem sharks, the hammerhead sharks, many of the smoothhound sharks, the wobbegongs, the nurse and whale sharks, the banded catsharks and some of the angelsharks. In the active group are the requiem, hammerhead and smoothhound sharks and the whale shark. These sharks swim almost continuously. They travel long distances every day and undertake seasonal migrations, in which they follow changes in water temperatures and currents.

ON THE REEFS
The silvertip shark is widespread in the topics from East Africa to Panama, but does not occur in the Atlantic. It is often found on seaward reefs at depths below 80 feet (25 m).

Larger active sharks Many larger members of these species—those that grow to more than 10 feet (3 m) long—are found in all the world's tropical waters. Examples are the tiger, bull, dusky, silky, whale and the three largest hammerhead sharks The bull shark is sometimes called the freshwater shark because it regularly enters freshwater rivers and lakes in most of its range around the world. In the Amazon River, it has been recorded more than 1,850 miles (3,000 km) upstream.

PLANKTON FEEDER
The whale shark is often found near the surface in tropical waters, where it filter feeds on plankton.

Smaller active sharks Smaller tropical marine sharks—less than 10 feet (3 m) long—tend to have smaller ranges. Many are restricted to the Indo-Pacific region. These include the winghead, whitetip reef, blacktip reef and gray reef sharks. Many smaller species—including the bonnethead, lemon and smalltail sharks—have populations in tropical coastal waters on either side of Central America. Such a distribution is probably due to an upheaval that occurred in the region about three million years ago in which a land barrier was thrown up, dividing what had previously been one uninterrupted expanse of sea.

LIMITED RANGE
The limited range of the winghead shark, which is restricted to the Indo-Pacific region, is typical of the range of many smaller active species.

Even smaller The smallest tropical sharks—less than 3 feet (1 m) long—include the blacktail reef, the Caribbean reef and Atlantic weasel sharks. These are often confined to very specific local areas.

45

BOTTOM-DWELLING TROPICAL SHARKS

The bottom-dwelling tropical sharks have, on the whole, relatively small ranges. They spend most of their time on the ocean floor, moving only to hunt their food. Indeed, many do not actively hunt. They simply sit, camouflaged, on the bottom waiting for a meal to come to them. When it does, they dart out, seize and devour it and then continue to wait.

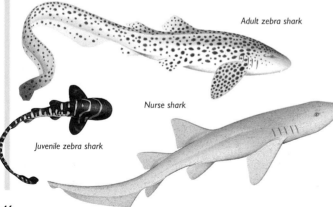

Adult zebra shark

Nurse shark

Juvenile zebra shark

Restricted range Data suggests that in their lifetimes, many bottom-dwellers do not travel more than a few miles from where they were born. Most tropical bottom-dwellers are fairly small, growing to no more than 6 feet (2 m) long. Most are restricted to a particular archipelago or small region. Examples of such sharks are the longtailed carpetsharks, wobbegongs and angelsharks.

Larger species Three species of fairly large bottom-dwelling sharks—the nurse, zebra and tawny nurse sharks—do not fit the above pattern. Being much larger sharks, growing on average to between 10 and 13 feet (3–4 m), they appear to travel much more than the smaller sharks. The zebra and tawny nurse sharks are found found throughout the Indo-Pacific region, ranging from South Africa, northward to the Red

LARGER BOTTOM-DWELLER
Coral reefs in tropical regions attract numerous shark species, including the docile tawny nurse shark. This is one of the larger of the bottom-dwelling tropical sharks, and can be a strong swimmer when it needs to be. It is found throughout the Indo-Pacific region.

and Arabian seas, and eastward along the coasts of India and China and across to Australia and even as far as Fiji. The nurse shark has an interesting distribution. In the eastern Atlantic it extends along the west coast of tropical Africa from around Senegal to Angola; in the western Atlantic it is found from the southern United States to Brazil, including the Caribbean and the Gulf of Mexico; and in the tropical eastern Pacific it is found from California to Peru.

Differences The three separate populations of nurse sharks are quite clearly distinguishable from each other, although the differences, in size and coloration, are not great enough to warrant calling them separate species. The western Atlantic and eastern Pacific nurse

sharks are more similar to each other than either is to the eastern Atlantic ones. This suggests that the western Atlantic and eastern Pacific sharks were separated when Central America arose between one and three million years ago and since then they have developed differently.

LONGTAILED CARPETSHARKS
The epaulette shark is one of at least 12 species of longtailed carpetsharks. These sharks are common inshore on coral and rocky reefs and in tide pools.

SHARKS OF THE PACIFIC REEFS

A typical Pacific reef has a shallow reef flat that separates the seaward reef from shallow backwaters or a lagoon. The backreef and lagoon are usually scattered with reefs of living coral across a sandy bottom. On the seaward side of the flat is the forereef, which falls off rapidly into deeper waters.

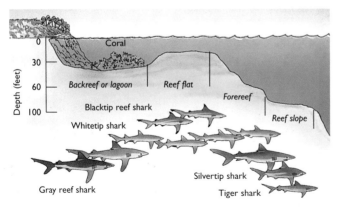

Blacktips and whitetips The species composition and distribution of sharks on different tropical reefs in the Pacific are remarkably similar. The blacktip reef shark, the most common shark on the reefs during the flood tide, feeds on a broad range of small fishes, crustaceans and cephalopods that inhabit the reef flat and adjacent shallow waters. This active species often moves around the reef in large aggregations, feeding mainly at night. The slightly larger whitetip reef shark tends to swim close to the bottom, where it moves

PACIFIC COMMUNITY

The species composition and distribution of sharks on tropical reefs of the Pacific are remarkably similar. The most common visitor to the reef flat is the blacktip reef shark, which sometimes frequents waters so shallow that its dorsal fin is exposed above the surface. The largest shark on most Pacific reefs is the tiger shark.

REEF VISITORS
Top: Blacktip sharks are found in all tropical and temperate waters. Near tropical reefs they usually stay in the deeper waters of the outer reef. Above: Tiger sharks, the largest sharks on Pacific reefs, can grow to more than 16 feet (5 m) long. They usually occur in deep water on the seaward side of reef flats, but individuals sometimes enter shallow waters adjacent to the reef flat to feed on seabirds at rest on the water.

mainly among reef crevices and caves. Only rarely is it observed on the reef flat or in very shallow waters. Studies have shown that individual whitetip reef sharks are strongly attached to specific geographical areas of the reef.

Gray reef shark The distribution of the gray reef shark overlaps considerably with that of the whitetip reef shark, but it is more abundant in deep areas on the seaward side of the reef, and also in deep areas of the backreef or lagoon. Its diet consists primarily of reef fishes and cephalopods. Like most other reef species, this shark does not seem to feed every day.

Voracious feeder The tiger shark, the largest shark on most reefs, has perhaps the most diverse diet of any shark. This diet ranges from large stingrays and other sharks to small fishes and bottom-dwelling crustaceans and cephalopods.

Because of its large size and wide-ranging habits, little is known of its movement patterns.

On the outer reef Other sharks commonly found on seaward reefs include the silvertip reef shark, which typically inhabits waters below 80 feet (25 m) and feeds on small fishes and mollusks; and the bull shark, blacktip shark and the various species of hammerheads.

IN THE REEF PASSES
The gray reef shark is one of the most common sharks on Indo-Pacific coral reefs. Divers often encounter these sharks in the reef passes. They must treat them with great caution as they are capable of unprovoked aggression.

TEMPERATE-WATER SHARKS

Temperate-water sharks live mostly at water temperatures between 50 and 70° Fahrenheit (10–21°C). As with tropical sharks, they can be divided into active swimmers and bottom-dwellers. Many active species are large sharks that are widely distributed. The bottom-dwellers are small and have a restricted range.

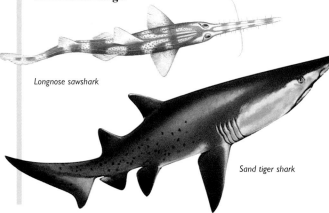

Longnose sawshark

Sand tiger shark

Moving about The active temperate-water sharks follow water currents or temperature changes. In winter they tend to be closer to the equator, and in summer farther away from it. Depending on the hemisphere, they will be farther north or farther south than tropical sharks. The larger species—more than 10 feet (3 m) long—are found virtually worldwide. However, they have what is called an antitropical distribution. This means that while they are in both hemispheres, they are generally absent in tropical or equatorial seas.

Venturing far and wide Widely distributed species include most of the lamnids: the basking, shortfin mako, great white and blue sharks, as well as the three thresher sharks and the sand tiger sharks. Some of these species range out of temperate

DIFFERENT RANGES

The great white shark (far left) and the blue shark (left) are two large sharks that range widely throughout temperate waters and even into tropical, and in the great white's case, cold-water regions. By contrast, the Port Jackson shark (below), like other bullhead sharks, is much more restricted by its limited diet.

waters into the deeper, cooler parts of tropical seas. The blue shark is probably one of the widest traveling species. Tagged individuals have been recorded as traveling from Long Island, New York, to Spain and from England to Brazil and New York.

Exclusive ranges Other temperate-water sharks also venture into tropical water, but to a lesser extent than the blue shark. Two lamnid species, the porbeagle and the salmon shark, have very similar and exclusive ranges. The salmon shark is found only in the cold and temperate waters of the northern Pacific Ocean. The porbeagle has an

amphitemperate distribution in the North and South Atlantic, the Indian Ocean and the southern fringes of the Pacific basin.

Smaller active sharks Smaller active temperate-water sharks have more limited ranges than the larger species. However, they too have populations in both hemispheres and are more or less absent in the tropics. Examples of these smaller active sharks are the piked dogfish, Cuban dogfish, Japanese spurdog, shortspine spurdog and the tope shark, as well as smoothhound sharks of the genus *Mustelus* and houndsharks of the species *Triakis*.

Bottom-dwellers Bottom-dwellers in temperate areas grow to less than 6 feet (2 m). They move very little and their distributions are quite limited. They are often restricted to small areas, such as a particular archipelago. Examples include angelsharks, sawsharks, bullhead sharks and many catsharks.

COLD-WATER SHARKS

Cold-water sharks inhabit waters colder than 50° Fahrenheit (10°C). Many of them live very far north or south, in or close to Arctic or Antarctic waters. Others live in the deep, cold waters of temperate, and even tropical, regions. Like tropical and temperate-water sharks, these swimmers can be divided into active swimmers and bottom-dwellers.

Larger active sharks Among the larger active cold-water sharks—more than 6 feet (2 m) long—are the sixgill and sevengill sharks, the frilled shark, false catshark, goblin shark and the sleeper sharks of the genus *Somniosus*. It is probable but not yet definitely established, that many of these sharks travel great distances, because food is relatively scarce in such cold waters.

SLUGGISH GIANT

The Greenland sleeper shark grows to 23 feet (7 m) long. It is the only polar shark in the Atlantic and has been recorded under polar icefloes. It is sluggish and shows little resistance when captured. Its distribution is shown in the map above.

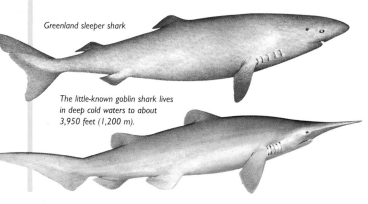

Greenland sleeper shark

The little-known goblin shark lives in deep cold waters to about 3,950 feet (1,200 m).

SIXGILL SHARK
The bluntnose sixgill shark is one of four species of sixgill sharks. They are large and stout-bodied, with comb-like teeth and distinctive green fluorescent eyes. These wide-ranging and worldwide sharks live on shelves and slopes from the surface to 6,500 feet (2,000 m).

Smaller active sharks Smaller active cold-water sharks—less than 3 feet (1 m) long—all live in depths of 1,000 feet (300 m) or more. Even in the far north and south they are not known to come close to the surface. At one time they were thought to be rather rare and to have very limited distributions. However, recent studies suggest that most of these species have global distributions in the deep sea. All the smaller active cold-water sharks are species of dogfish sharks.

Bottom-dwellers Bottom-dwelling cold-water sharks are found only in deep cold waters and never come close to the surface, even in the far north or south. Most are less than 3 feet (1 m) in length but, unlike the active swimming species, have small distributions. They seem to be sedentary and to move only short distances during their entire lives. Although the deepwater catsharks (genus *Apristurus*) are worldwide in distribution, and the five species of roughsharks are fairly widespread, all the other cold-water bottom-dwellers (there are at least 31 species) seem to have their own "pockets" on the ocean floor. The exception is the false catshark, which grows to between 6 and 10 feet (2–3 m) long, and which seems to be reasonably widespread.

Broadnose sevengill shark (above) and frilled shark (below)

SHARKS OF DEEP MIDWATERS

Below the euphotic zone, at depths of 650 feet (200 m), the sea is dark and is without the sun-driven photosynthesis that supports most life on Earth. Animals in this zone depend for their sustenance on dead and decaying plants and animals that drift down from lesser depths, or they venture to the surface to find their food.

The blackbelly lanternshark is widespread on or near the bottom of outer continental shelves.

The crocodile shark moves from the surface to depths of 1,970 feet (600 m).

Large eyes and camouflage

Many small sharks from the dogfish family (Squalidae) ascend at dusk to the surface to feed and return at dawn to the safety of the deep midwaters. They rely on their large eyes—a feature of most deepwater species—and good vision to find their prey. They also use their ventral bioluminescence to camouflage themselves from potential predators and to disguise themselves from fish they intend to prey upon.

Blackbelly lanternshark

The blackbelly lanternshark is one of more than 17 species of lanternsharks, so named because they produce their own camouflaging light. These sharks have numerous, minute bioluminescent (light-producing) photophores along the underside of their bodies. The light from the photophores is a means of camouflage because it "counter-illuminates" the shark. The shark produces just enough weak light on the underside of its body to equal the amount of down-welling light between it and the ocean's surface. Because of this optical illusion, it merges with the ocean and cannot be seen by potential predators—or by unsuspecting prey. The blackbelly lanternshark is widespread on outer continental shelves. It lives on or near the bottom at depths between 590 and 2,700 feet (180–835 m) and is found mainly in southern oceans. This small, stocky shark, which grows to a maximum length of 16 inches (40 cm), is closely related to the dwarf lanternshark, which is a mere 8 inches (20 cm) long and is probably the smallest living shark.

Cookiecutter The deep waters of the open sea are home to many small predatory sharks that have developed special features and behaviors to enable them to prey on the

The piked dogfish is a coastal species and ranges from shallow water to 2,600 feet (800 m).

organisms that live in their habitat. One of these is the cookiecutter shark, which has specialized suctorial jaws and lips and razor-sharp, saw-like lower teeth. These allow it to cut oval-shaped plugs of tissue (like a cookiecutter cutting pastry) from its victims, which include large marlins, tunas and seals. This tropical shark normally inhabits depths as great as 11,500 feet (3,570 m), but has been observed, and caught, at the surface. Like the lanternsharks, it has bioluminescent light organs which glow in the dark and lure prey.

Crocodile shark The crocodile has long, thin, needle-like teeth, similar to those of the large mako sharks, with which it seizes its midwater prey, which includes shrimp, lanternfishes and squid. It is probably a fast-swimming predator that chases small prey, either near the surface at night or down to 1,000 feet (300 m) in the mesapelagic zone during the day.

Piked dogfish These cold-water sharks do not live exclusively in deep water. Large schools of them routinely frequent the shallow and coastal waters of higher latitudes in spring and fall, and migrate into deep waters during the cooler winter months.

SHARKS OF THE DEEP BOTTOMS

Some sharks live in the abyss, that portion of the ocean that is below the continental slope and covered by 13,000 feet (4 km) of sea water. Because of the inaccessibility of this environment, some of the sharks that live there have been little studied.

The gigantic, slow-moving Pacific sleeper shark inhabits temperate to cold waters.

The prickly dogfish lives at depths of 165 to 1,640 feet (50–500 m).

Cold and dark For sharks such as the lumbering sleeper sharks and the gulper dogfishes that inhabit the deep bottoms, their habitat is a cold place, usually 31 to 39° Fahrenheit (-0.6–4°C). It is almost completely dark, except for the light made by animals, such as those sharks that have bioluminescent light organs. Adaptations at such depths require the ability to find and capture food, to avoid being eaten and to find a mate—in the dark.

Huge and sluggish Two giants of the deep, members of the genus *Somniosus*, are the Greenland and the Pacific sleeper sharks which grow respectively to 23 feet (7 m) and 15 feet (4.6 m) long. The Greenland sleeper is an Atlantic species, while the Pacific sleeper is found in the northern Pacific Ocean, as far north as the Siberian coast. In most of its range it lives at great depths, but in the coldest waters it comes into shallow areas. Though sluggish swimmers, both are able to catch large, swift-moving prey.

Migrating midget The spined pygmy shark, a tiny deepwater dogfish, is almost as small as the dwarf lanternshark, the world's

56

smallest shark. Its size could make it an easy prey for larger predators, but luminous photophores on its underside camouflage it from would-be attackers. Like some other deepwater sharks, it makes a nightly visit to the surface in order to feed.

OASES IN THE DEEP

In places on the deep ocean floor, miles below the surface, volcanic activity allows water to percolate down beneath the sea floor to be superheated and return as a fountain of hot water gushing forth into the ice-cold darkness of the abyss. These vents form oases in the deep sea.

Chemical activity in the vent forms hydrogen sulfide. Bacteria use this as an energy source to make food.

Near the vent grow clams up to 12 inches (30 cm) long.

Several little-known fish species inhabit the fringes of the community.

HOW SHARKS WORK

From swift and powerful swimmers in the open ocean to slow-moving dwellers on the seabed, and ranging in size from massive to minute, sharks are biologically diverse and sophisticated animals. They have streamlined bodies, complex arrangements of fins and flexible cartilaginous skeletons. These features combine with an efficient respiratory system and a dazzling array of sensory organs—some of them still not well understood by scientists—to give them an impressive mastery of the watery environment that they inhabit.

SHARK ANATOMY

A shark's internal organs have many unique features. The body has a cartilaginous skeleton, consisting of a braincase (enclosing the brain, inner ears, eyes and nasal organs); a long vertebral column; paired cartilages that support the jaws, tongue and gill arches; girdles that support the pectoral and pelvic fins; and the fin skeletons.

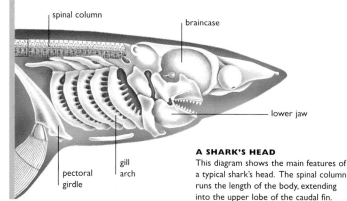

spinal column

braincase

lower jaw

pectoral girdle

gill arch

A SHARK'S HEAD
This diagram shows the main features of a typical shark's head. The spinal column runs the length of the body, extending into the upper lobe of the caudal fin.

Inside a shark A shark's body includes two cavities: the pericardial cavity, just below the gills, which contains the heart; and the trunk, or visceral, cavity, which begins below the esophagus and contains other internal organs. The head and trunk enclose a tubular gut, which includes the digestive system. This tubular gut begins in the head at the mouth and ends at the vent, or excretory opening, between the pelvic fins. The mouth opens into the pharynx, which is connected, via the esophagus, to the stomach.

The visceral cavity The stomach often extends through part or all of the visceral cavity and then doubles back, connecting to the first part of the intestine, or duodenum, by way of a tubular section known as the pylorus. This attaches to the valvular intestine, which in turn extends to the rectum. The rectum discharges solid waste into the cloaca and this waste is expelled through the vent. The visceral cavity also contains a central gall bladder and the liver, which is often very large and extends rearward to fill the lower part of the visceral cavity.

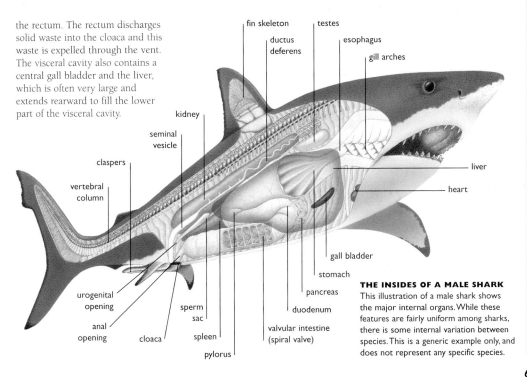

fin skeleton

ductus deferens

testes

esophagus

gill arches

kidney

seminal vesicle

claspers

vertebral column

liver

heart

gall bladder

stomach

pancreas

duodenum

valvular intestine (spiral valve)

urogenital opening

anal opening

sperm sac

spleen

cloaca

pylorus

THE INSIDES OF A MALE SHARK
This illustration of a male shark shows the major internal organs. While these features are fairly uniform among sharks, there is some internal variation between species. This is a generic example only, and does not represent any specific species.

BREATHING UNDERWATER

Sharks breathe by extracting dissolved oxygen from water that passes through their gills. At the same time, metabolic wastes, such as carbon dioxide, are discharged into the water. Typically, water enters the mouth cavity, or pharynx, flows through the internal gill openings into the gills and is expelled through the external gill openings, or gill slits.

How gills work The gills (or branchial region) consist of the skeletons of the gill and tongue arches; associated muscles that operate the gill pump; and the skin, blood vessels and connective tissue which make up the gill septa and gill

RESPIRATION
Left: When open to expel deoxygenated water, the large external openings of a whale shark clearly reveal the thin, plate-like gill filaments inside.
Above right: Active pelagic sharks often rely on forward movement to force water through their gills.

filaments. Gill filaments are thin, plate-like structures, arranged in line with the flow of water through the gill cavities. They have a rich supply of blood vessels, and play a vital role in supplying oxygen to all parts of the body and in diffusing dissolved wastes into the water.

Water through the gills To absorb enough oxygen, sharks need to maintain a good flow of water over their gills. Some sharks generate much of this flow through constant forward movement—a process known as ram ventilation. Some highly active species, such as mackerel sharks and some requiem sharks, rely almost solely on this process to breathe during their normal activities.

The gill pump While ram ventilation is effective for sharks that are constantly on the move, most species are less active, spending at least some of the time resting on the bottom or hovering motionless. These sharks supplement ram ventilation by means of an active, muscular gill pump. This works like a set of bellows, taking water into the pharynx and pumping it through the gills. Water enters the mouth as the muscles of the tongue and gill arches depress the mouth, increasing its capacity. Other muscles then close the mouth and contract the pharynx, forcing water out through the internal gill openings. External muscles on the gills then contract, forcing the water to squeeze through the gill filaments and out the external gill openings. The cycle is then repeated over and over.

HOW A SHARK BREATHES
Water enters the mouth, passes over the gills and out through the gill slits. This cutaway diagram shows how the water and blood flow in opposite directions through the shark's respiratory system.

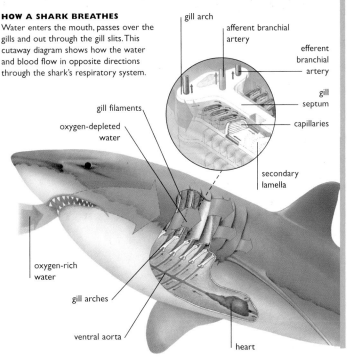

gill arch

afferent branchial artery

efferent branchial artery

gill septum

capillaries

gill filaments

oxygen-depleted water

secondary lamella

oxygen-rich water

gill arches

ventral aorta

heart

SHARK SENSES

The traditional five senses—touch, taste, smell, sight and hearing—are well developed in sharks. Sharks also have several other less familiar senses. Where sharks excel is in the variety and complexity of their sense organs and in the integration of sensory information within their nervous system to produce a complex picture of their world.

Erroneous assumptions Even today, sharks are often presented as sluggish, instinctive and random predators that possess poorly developed sensory systems and rudimentary brains. This view stems

from their long fossil history, and the assumption that they are less advanced than the more recently evolved vertebrates. Nothing could be further from the truth.

Swimming noses Early attempts to understand how sharks perceived their environment concentrated on the sense of smell. Nineteenth-century biologists plugged the nasal openings in sharks' snouts and observed that they then failed to detect food. As a result, scientists concluded that sharks were

essentially "swimming noses," and that the other senses were of only minor importance. We now know that feeding behaviors depend upon a range of important senses, including one—electroreception—that is absent or poorly understood in most other animals.

A SHARK'S SENSES

The diagrams on the right-hand page show the components of a shark's sensory systems for vision, smell, taste and touch and where they are located on the body. The text on the following pages gives an explanation of how each of these senses functions as well as information about hearing—which, despite the lack of external evidence of ears, is very acute—and electrosense.

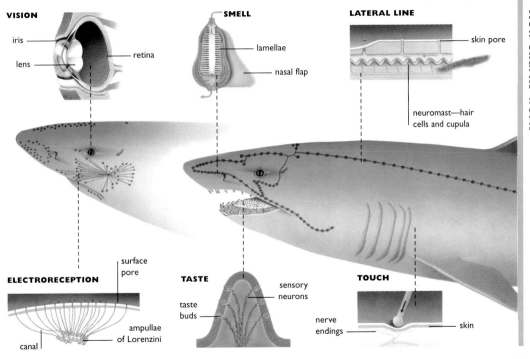

VISION
- iris
- lens
- retina

SMELL
- lamellae
- nasal flap

LATERAL LINE
- skin pore
- neuromast—hair cells and cupula

ELECTRORECEPTION
- surface pore
- ampullae of Lorenzini
- canal

TASTE
- sensory neurons
- taste buds

TOUCH
- nerve endings
- skin

SHARK SENSES: EARS AND EYES

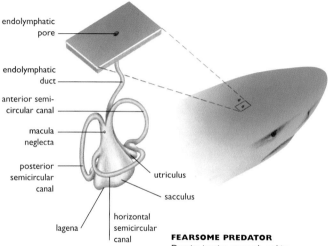

endolymphatic pore

endolymphatic duct

anterior semi-circular canal

macula neglecta

posterior semicircular canal

utriculus

sacculus

lagena

horizontal semicircular canal

Ears As with other vertebrates, the sense of hearing in sharks is localized in the paired inner ears. These are buried inside the braincase and lie alongside the rear of the brain. The inner ears are also a shark's principal organs of balance and coordination. The system that controls balance is known as the vestibular system. Inside each ear are three fluid-filled semicircular canals. As the shark moves and turns, the ear detects low-level compression waves (sound) in water and regulates balance by detecting the motion of

VESTIBULAR SYSTEM
A shark's vestibular system, in each of its middle ears, involves three semicircular canals, filled with fluid and situated at right angles to each other.

FEARSOME PREDATOR
Despite its size, strength and its razor-sharp teeth, the great white would not be the fearsome predator that it is without its keenly attuned senses of hearing, sight and smell. These, combined with its well-developed electrosensory capacity, enable it to locate and track down its prey.

While most sharks have immovable eyelids, some, including catsharks, have a movable eyelid known as a nictitating membrane. This moves upward to protect the eye while the shark feeds.

The bigeye thresher, a deepwater dweller, is noted for its huge eyes.

the fluid within the canals. Inner ears can also detect the pull of gravity and changes in velocity and direction as the shark swims.

Hearing Hearing in sharks is apparently directional, which may help them find struggling or injured fishes that are emitting sounds, or potential prey that have natural sound-producing organs. The inner ears of some inshore sharks are apparently sensitive to compression waves in the water at much lower frequencies than the human ear can detect. These sharks can detect sounds of 10 to 800 hertz (cycles per second). Human ears range from

about 25 to 16,000 hertz. Some sharks react to loud underwater sounds produced several miles away.

Sight Shark's eyes are positioned on the sides of the head. This allows them a wider range of vision than many other animals. Relatively inactive sharks that inhabit shallow waters—such as carpetsharks—have eyes that are significantly smaller than those of other species. This suggests that they rely far less upon vision than do other species. More active midwater species have larger eyes. Extremely large eye size is typical of deep-dwelling sharks. The basic structure of a shark's eye is broadly similar to the eye structure of other vertebrates.

The frilled shark, another deepwater dweller, has relatively large eyes.

The shortnose sawshark has eyes close together near the top of its flattened snout.

SHARK SENSES: SMELL, TOUCH AND TASTE

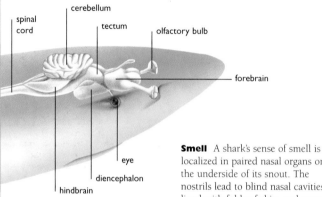

spinal cord

cerebellum

tectum

olfactory bulb

forebrain

eye

diencephalon

hindbrain

A SHARK'S BRAIN

A shark's sensory systems are centered in the brain. The hindbrain processes much sensory information; the cerebellum coordinates body movements; the tectum receives visual and electrosensory information; and the forebrain receives information from the olfactory and electrosensory systems.

Smell A shark's sense of smell is localized in paired nasal organs on the underside of its snout. The nostrils lead to blind nasal cavities lined with folds of skin, and sensory cells on these folds are capable of detecting chemicals in water. As a shark swims, water passes into the nasal cavity through the forward-facing nostril openings, passes the sensory folds and exits through rear-facing outlets. When sharks are at rest, the respiratory current entering the mouth tends to draw a stream of water into the nostrils. Sharks are renowned for their olfactory acuity and most species have large to huge olfactory organs. They are able to determine the direction of an attractive scent in water. The maximum distance over which sharks can track a sense is likely to be many miles.

Touch The sense of touch is the least understood of all the shark's senses. We do know, however, that the senses of touch, temperature

BARBELS AND NOSTRILS
Angelsharks (above) are masters of disguise. Their barbels may be organs of touch or smell. The nostrils and eyes of a hammerhead (left) are at the opposite tips of its distinctive head.

detection, and possibly pain detection are localized in sense organs in the skin. Sharks respond to external physical contact, presumably from skin sense organs, but also from lateral line and pit organs (see page 70). They also have stretch-reception organs in the skin. Known as proprioceptors, these respond to the movement of skin and muscles. They can be used to fine-tune body movements, particularly those of the fins and jaws, by feeding back information to the brain.

Taste A shark's sense of taste is localized in specialized clusters of cells (taste buds) on the papillae of the roof and floor of the pharynx and the tongue. Taste is little understood in sharks, but presumably functions when they ingest food and other items. Experiments with free-ranging requiem sharks suggest that they have a well-developed ability to discriminate between tastes. When presented with similar baits from sea bass and certain marine mollusks, the sharks initially took all the baits into their mouths, but consistently spat out the mollusks. Similar experiments with captive requiem sharks suggest that they actively discriminate between the meat of different fishes, choosing only those that they find palatable. Apart from its role in food selection, taste may also be involved in detecting differences in salinity in the water.

SAFE HITCHHIKER
The shark's senses are well attuned to detect and catch prey, but remoras, even though they attach themselves to the shark's gill cavities and skin, are immune from attack. They do the shark a service by removing harmful parasites.

ELECTROSENSE AND LATERAL LINE

In addition to the five senses humans and many other animals use to observe and respond to their world, sharks have other senses that are difficult for us to understand. These include senses for experiencing weak vibrations in the water and for detecting weak electric fields (electrosense).

IN SEARCH OF PREY

Electrosense is one powerful tool at the disposal of the crested bullhead shark, as it seeks out sea urchins, seastars, barnacles, marine worms and other small marine creatures in the sandy seabed.

The lateral line The lateral line is a pair of sensory tubes that extends beneath the skin from the head to the base of the caudal fin, along the flanks and tail. On the head, the lateral line extends over the eyes, across the top of the head, below the eyes, on the cheeks and on the snout. The main tubes have pores, or smaller tubes, connecting them to the exterior surface of the skin. Inside the tubes are sets of sensory cells with hair-like protrusions (known as neuromasts) that react when the hairs are stimulated by

SENSES COMBINED

This sand tiger is clearly searching for food, but exactly what combination of senses it is using is difficult to say. However, electrosense plays a part. The ampullae of Lorenzini are often visible as clusters of dark pores around a shark's snout and jaws.

movement and pressure. Related to the lateral system, but lacking internal tubes, are the pit organs. These are blind pockets in the skin with sensory hair cells inside them. They are scattered over the body and guarded by pairs of denticles.

The lateral line of sharks is an important means for detecting water movements made by prey and potential predators.

Electrosense Sharks are sensitive to weak electric fields, and this electrosense is localized in specialized sense organs in their heads. These are known as ampullae of Lorenzini and are located below the skin in the snout, lips and just behind the eyes. The ampullae are sense organs that contain receptor cells in a cluster of open cavities or pockets. These have a common connection to jelly-filled, elongated tubes that extend to pores on the skin's surface. Together, the ampullae, tubes and pores are termed ampullary organs. They probably have a number of functions. Most importantly, they enable a shark to detect and locate prey, but only over small distances. The weak bioelectric stimuli produced by prey originate primarily from their biological membranes and appear to a shark as a weak electrical aura around them, even when the prey is buried in sand.

canal

neuromasts

surface pore

main tube

LATERAL LINE
This shows the extent of a shark's lateral line system. The cutaway detail shows how vibrations enter through the pores and stimulate the sensory hair cells, or neuromasts, that are connected to the shark's nervous system.

lateral line

TAILS

The tail, or caudal fin, of a shark is the main means of propulsion through the water. In most sharks, the tail generates forward thrust by swinging from side to side, creating an undulation of the body. Special connective tissue fibers under the skin transfer much of the body's power directly to the tail.

Different shapes and sizes

According to the species, shark's tails differ greatly in size and shape. In all cases, however, sharks' caudal fins have two lobes and in almost every instance, the upper lobe is conspicuously larger than the lower one. The size and shape of its caudal fin is often a key to a shark's pattern of activity—or inactivity.

Inactive deepwater sharks

In all living sharks, the vertebral column extends into the caudal fin. In the case of bottom-dwelling sharks and those that float in deep water, the vertebral column is nearly straight (or directed downward in angelsharks) and the lower caudal lobe is low. Nurse sharks, which spend most of their time on the ocean floor, where they sleep during the day, have only a tiny lower lobe.

WHALE AND WHITETIP
The view from behind of a whale shark (above) is dominated by its huge, powerful caudal fin. It needs a massive tail to propel its massive body forward. The fins and tails of oceanic whitetip sharks (left) have conspicuous, mottled white tips.

They swim along the seabed by moving their bodies in a rather eel-like manner and sweeping their tails slowly from side to side.

Active sharks In active sharks, on the other hand, the vertebral column is elevated into the caudal fin, which is high and more or less crescent-shaped (much like those of swift-swimming tunas or swordfishes). The upper lobe of the caudal fin in thresher sharks is greatly elongated and sickle-shaped and is used as a whip for stunning prey as well as for swimming. The zebra shark also has a greatly elongated tail, which is low and strap-like, but why it is so elongated is not known.

Bursts of speed The tiger shark's tail is well adapted to its predatory patterns. The tail is epiceral (the upper lobe is longer and heavier than the lower lobe). This species swims by swinging its body from side to side, and the large upper

VARIATIONS ON A THEME

Closest to ancestral form are the the tails of tiger and nurse sharks, with their long upper lobes—a feature that is extreme in the thresher shark. The porbeagle's short, more symmetrical tail is versatile, suited to slow cruising punctuated by sudden bursts of speed. The cookiecutter's tail is typical of an active deepwater shark.

lobe delivers the maximum amount of power for slow cruising or sudden bursts of speed in pursuit of prey. The tiger shark's varied diet means that it must be able to twist and turn rapidly when hunting turtles, fishes, stingrays and other sharks. Porbeagles use their tails for propulsion rather than swinging their bodies from side to side. The large lower lobe of the caudal fin provides greater speed after fast-moving prey, and lateral "keels" at the base of the tail may reduce drag for efficient hunting. Great whites, close relatives of porbeagles, have nearly symmetrical tails, which are capable of enormous thrust.

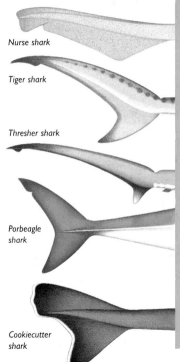

Nurse shark

Tiger shark

Thresher shark

Porbeagle shark

Cookiecutter shark

FINS

Like their tails, or caudal fins, the fins of different sharks vary enormously in size and shape, but they all serve a common purpose—to help the sharks maintain balance as they swim and to control the direction and speed of their movements.

Paired and unpaired fins All species of sharks have two sets of paired fins on the lower part of their bodies—the pectoral fins near the front and the pelvic fins, situated farther back. They also have between two and four unpaired fins: the caudal fin, or tail; one or, in most cases, two dorsal fins, situated on the top of the body; and, in just over two-thirds of shark species, an anal fin, usually the smallest fin. In some cases, but not the majority, the dorsal fins have spines on them.

Fins and movement The variety of movements of which a shark is capable with its full complement of fins is complex and not well studied. What is apparent is that the coordinated action of the fins and body are fluid, precise and extremely well integrated. A shark's fins provide lift, braking and turning power, acceleration and tracking, and prevent pitch, roll and yaw. It has been postulated that the typical body form of sharks is an adaptation for cruising, a requirement of their predatory way of life. In the typical

SPINES OR NO SPINES

The presence or absence of spines on species that have two dorsal fins is an important distinguishing feature. The whale shark (far left) and the Port Jackson shark (left) both have two dorsal fins. The whale shark has no spines. The Port Jackson, however, is distinguished by its dorsal fin spines.

**BLACKTIPS
AND SILVERTIPS**
The blacktip reef shark
(below) is easily recognized
by the very distinct black
marks on its fins, especially
the first dorsal and caudal
fins. It is different from the
blacktip shark, which is a
larger species with thin black
tips on most of its fins. The
silvertip shark (left) has
distinctive white tips and
margins on all its fins.

shark, the placement of the pectoral
and dorsal fins probably results in
poor acceleration, but the spacing
between them is critical in
interacting with the water flow to
increase efficiency and thrust.

Fin structure Sharks' fins have
streamlined cross-sections, thick and
rounded in front and tapering to a
fine edge at the rear. In many sharks,
the pectoral and pelvic fins are
additionally convex on top and
concave below, providing lift as the
shark moves forward. Shark fins
generally have a rear notch and a free
rear tip that can be moved sideways
(in the case of dorsal and anal fins)
or up and down (in the case of
pectoral and pelvic fins). The fins
themselves are flexible and
have internal
muscles that
allow them
to bend and
tilt while the shark
is maneuvering
or braking.

JAWS

The energy that sharks need for activities such as swimming must ultimately come from the food they catch, and sharks owe much of their success as effective predators to the efficiency and diversity of their feeding mechanisms—their jaws and teeth. Shark jaws are simple, consisting basically of upper and lower jaw cartilages.

Jaw development In the most primitive of known sharks, the cladodonts, the mouth was terminal (at the front of the head) rather than ventral (underslung), and the long jaws consisted of a single upper and lower jaw cartilage. The upper jaw was bound to the cranium by ligaments which allowed little independent movement. Cladodont sharks were probably active pelagic predators, but their long jaws and pointed teeth were adapted to seizing and tearing prey rather than to cutting or sawing as in modern forms. In the later hybodont sharks the jaw shortened, allowing for a more powerful bite, and the teeth became modified for cutting and crushing. The most important change in sharks' jaws was the freeing of the upper jaw from the cranium. This made the upper jaw more mobile and enabled the shark to protrude its jaws. The ventral position of the jaws of modern sharks resulted from further shortening of the jaws, together with expansion of the snout, which could then take on a sensory function.

KEEPING TROPHIES
Game fishers are proud of their victories over "fighting" sharks such as great whites, makos and threshers and often preserve their catches' jaws to commemorate a struggle that may have lasted several hours.

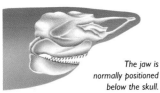

The jaw is normally positioned below the skull.

The jaw remains close to the skull as the mouth opens.

The upper jaw detaches from the skull.

Modern jaws In modern sharks the upper jaw is loosely suspended under the skull and is connected to the lower jaw at the outer rear corners. The upper jaw often overlaps the lower jaw in an overbite. While modern sharks have mobile upper jaws, the amount of mobility varies. Hornsharks and carpetsharks have grooves in the skull, along which the jaws slide forward. In other species, such as the great white shark, the jaws are more mobile. As it attacks, its jaws move downward and are simultaneously thrust forward. The jaw cartilages of sharks vary in shape. Sharks with small teeth usually have slender jaws; those with large cutting teeth tend to have deep, stout jaws.

JAWS AND BITES

The diagrams above show how a typical shark's jaw detaches from the skull as the shark attacks its prey.

Below we see stages in the biting action of a great white shark: in stage 1, the mouth begins to open; in stage 2, the snout lifts as the upper jaw protrudes; in stage 3, the lower jaw slips forward; and in stage 4, it closes again on the prey.

Stage 1

Stage 2

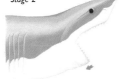

Stage 3

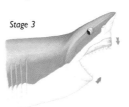

Stage 4

TEETH

A shark's teeth are more than just weapons. They are versatile manipulatory organs and, in the absence of tentacles, arms or fingers, they, along with the jaws are a shark's primary means of interacting with the environment. While they are mainly feeding organs, they are also used in social interactions, as well as in defense.

DIFFERENT BITES
The sand tiger (above) has long, sharp teeth that have become adapted for grasping and impaling large fishes. The bottlenose dolphin (left) is the victim of a cookiecutter's bite. This shark forms a suction cap with its lips, then bites and swivels round to cut out a plug of tissue.

Varieties of teeth As far as we know, sharks feed entirely on other animals, from tiny plankton to large whales. This variety is reflected in the wide range of tooth shapes found in modern sharks.

Long, thin teeth A primitive type of tooth found in many fossil sharks has a single slender cusp, a number of smaller cusps either side of it and a long, flat base. Similar teeth are still found in certain modern sharks (such as frilled sharks and sand tiger sharks) that consume small fishes and other animals. These sharks use their long, thin teeth to impale their prey before eating them whole.

Serrated teeth Many species of shark attack prey that is too large to be eaten whole, tearing off chunks of

flesh instead. The great white and tiger sharks have huge, broad, serrated teeth superbly suited to this feeding strategy. Many dogfish sharks have small, overlapping, compressed, sharp-edged teeth in the lower, and sometimes upper, jaws.

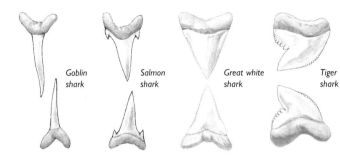

Goblin shark *Salmon shark* *Great white shark* *Tiger shark*

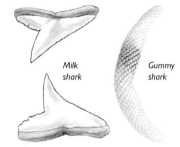

Milk shark *Gummy shark*

Together these function like a sawblade and can be used to cut out chunks of prey. Cookiecutter sharks have large, saw-like cutting teeth in their lower jaw. When they bite, these sharks suck onto the prey with their lips and swivel around, removing a plug of flesh. Other species, such as the dusky shark, combine broad cutting teeth in the upper jaw with long, thin, gripping teeth in the lower jaw—an arrangement ideal for catching large fishes, sharks and rays.

Bottom-dwellers and filter feeders Bottom-dwellers that feed on hard-shelled invertebrates have specialized teeth for crushing shells. In the case of smoothhounds and hornsharks, the cusps on some or all of their teeth are greatly reduced or absent. These low, flattened teeth can be used as a mill to crush the shark's hard-shelled prey. Filter feeders, such as whale sharks, have small, hook-like teeth. These are not used for feeding but may have a role in social interactions.

AN ARRAY OF SHAPES

These pictures give some idea of the variety of shark teeth shapes—from the long, impaling teeth of the goblin shark to the flat pavement-like patterns of the gummy shark's teeth, which are designed to crush rather than cut prey.

Replacing teeth Shark teeth have a short life and are replaced as they break or become worn. Experiments with captive lemon sharks and hornsharks suggest that a tooth lasts from under a month to about a year.

SCALES AND SKIN

A shark's skin affords the shark protection from infection and damage. It provides streamlining; plays a role in camouflage and display; and produces scales, teeth, spines, sense organs, glands and their secretions.

Thickness and strength While a shark's skin is often only a fraction of an inch thick and is relatively tough, there is much variation between species. In some deepwater gulper sharks and lanternsharks, the skin is thin and papery, while in the case of mature whale sharks the skin can be more than an inch (2.5 cm) thick and very tough.

Composition Shark skin is richly supplied with nerves, blood vessels and sense organs. It consists of an outer layer (epidermis) with multiple layers of cells, and an inner layer (dermis) comprised of cells in a network of tissue fibers. Pigment cells (chromatophores) are in the dermis, while glandular cells and multicellular glands occur in the epidermis. Specialized glandular cells are present in the sheaths of skin around the fin spines of dogfish sharks, and these produce toxins that can cause pain or even allergic shock to humans or potential predators.

WOBBEGONG
Like all six species of wobbegongs, the spotted wobbegong has elaborately patterned skin. Wobbegongs are common on rocky and coral reefs around the Australian coast and their cryptic coloration provides perfect camouflage.

The color pattern of the epaulette shark (left) is designed for camouflage. So too is the skin of the Pacific angelshark, which lies disguised on the sandy bottom. The bramble shark gets its name from its prominent spine-like denticles. The spines on each of a hornshark's dorsal fins are formed by secretions from the inner and outer skin layers.

Deepwater sharks have luminous organs (photophores) in their skin. These contain light-producing cells and cells that work as lenses. Together these function like miniature flashlights.

Plate-like scales Plate-like scales, or dermal denticles, are anchored in the skin and protrude from it. These are protective and generally cover the entire external surface of the body as well as all, or part of, the fins and mouth cavity. Denticles are periodically shed as new ones grow out through the skin. In bottom-dwelling sharks, denticles are often

rough and enlarged, but in many oceanic sharks they are small, with parallel ridges on their crowns.

Body markings Sharks' color and body markings derive from pigment cells in the dermis. In general, sharks tend to be dull-colored. Their color patterns allow them to blend with their surroundings and conceal them from enemies and prey. Pelagic sharks usually have dark upper bodies and are white below. Deep-water sharks are often dark brown or black, while inshore bottom-dwellers often have mottled, spotted color patterns that blend with reefs.

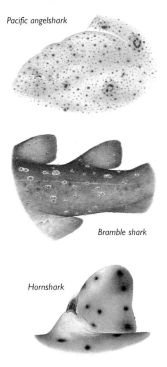

Pacific angelshark

Bramble shark

Hornshark

SHARK
BEHAVIOR

The long-standing myth that sharks are nothing more than mindless, destructive automatons has been disproved by studies that show them to be sophisticated and intelligent animals, capable of learning and possessing a range of often complex social behavior patterns that we still do not fully understand. These are related to feeding, defense, mating, reproduction and migration. As advanced technologies tap into the ocean's secrets, we are gradually building up a picture of the way sharks exploit and interact with their aquatic environment.

FEEDING

Contrary to popular belief, sharks are not scavengers of the deep, feeding indiscriminately on garbage or anything that crosses their path. Although few species have been studied in detail, it seems that sharks eat only what they need in order to survive, grow and reproduce.

The shark's diet Sharks are carnivores and consume a wide variety of food, ranging from microscopic zooplankton to whales. Active hunting sharks feed mainly on bony fishes, cephalopods and

crustaceans. Large active sharks may also eat rays, turtles, dolphins, seals and even other sharks. Some sharks, including smaller bottom-dwellers, hunt on the seabed for invertebrates, such as crustaceans, worms, mollusks and echinoderms. The tiger shark is probably the only shark that could justifiably be called a "trash

A VARIED DIET
The whale shark's diet is more varied than that of some other filter feeders, and includes small fishes such as sardines and anchovies and even larger fishes, such as mackerel, as well as crustacean plankton.

can of the sea." As well as almost any animal it can capture (including seals and sea birds), this opportunistic feeder will eat carrion washed down flooded rivers and has even been known to consume pieces of plastic and other garbage.

Locating and capturing prey
Sharks use many of their senses to find and capture their prey and are able to detect healthy, wounded, dying or dead fish over long distances. It is presumed that they are able to home in on scent trails provided by healthy animals. Odors from dead or bleeding animals travel many miles on ocean currents and sharks follow these trails until they locate their prey. Wounded fishes send out distinctive low-frequency sounds that sharks can detect. Vision can play an important role once sharks are within about 65 feet

The whale shark's huge mouth can be a place of sanctuary. Fishes sometimes "voluntarily" swim inside, running the risk of being swallowed, but finding there temporary shelter from other, more aggressive, predators.

Waiting for food Some sharks, such as well-camouflaged wobbegongs and angelsharks, lie motionless on the ocean floor, waiting in ambush for prey. When a fish ventures too close, the shark will open its mouth, drawing in water and the prey. The water is expelled through the gill openings and strong, backward-facing, needle-like teeth trap the prey, which is consumed whole. Whale and basking sharks are filter feeders, concentrating on swarms of plankton. They do not use their teeth to capture prey. Their gills have long, thin extensions (gill rakers) that form a fine mesh to filter plankton from the water. The sharks may swim vertically through these swarms until they reach the surface.

(20 m) of their prey. The electrical and olfactory senses of some species play a primary role in locating prey. Small hammerheads have been observed sweeping their heads back and forth across the ocean floor in search of small fishes hidden there. The sharks can detect the odors of the fishes as well as locate the electrical impulses they emit.

Disabling prey Sharks will often disable their prey before consuming it. For example, great white sharks feeding on sea lions around the Farallon Islands, off the coast of California, have been observed biting a sea lion, then waiting until it dies from the massive wound before consuming it. This reduces the risk of being injured by the sea lion.

FEEDING continued

Learning where to look

Evidence suggests that sharks can learn and remember where to find food. Every fall, whale sharks appear off Western Australia's Ningaloo Reef to coincide with the mass spawning of coral and other reef animals, which generates an explosion in the number of plankton. Similarly, tiger sharks enter the waters around the French Frigate Shoals off the northwest Hawaiian Islands every year as young black-footed albatrosses learn to fly. Birds that crash into the ocean are quickly attacked and eaten. Sharks have also learned to take advantage of the habits of humans with many regularly following fishing boats, waiting for old bait or unwanted fishes to be discarded. Dive operators capitalize on such learning behavior to entice shark to specific locations with regular supplies of bait.

ATTRACTED BY BAIT

Above: A group of gray reef sharks swarm around bait at the end of an angler's line in a furious feeding frenzy. Such feeding behavior is rare in the wild.
Right: This great white shark has learned that food is always to be had at a place regularly visited by a boat operator who takes tourists on expeditions to view sharks in the wild.

Food requirements The energy requirement of sharks varies greatly between species. Captive bull and blue sharks on average consume 0.5 and 0.6 percent respectively of their body weight per day. Mako sharks have the highest energy requirements because of an active nature and high body temperature. They consume about 3 percent of their body weight per day. Juvenile sharks also have high food intakes to support rapid growth rates. Sharks do not need to feed daily. A shark's stomach will hold around 10 percent of its body weight, so if large prey is consumed the shark may need to feed only once or twice a week. Sharks that consume small prey must feed more regularly, possibly twice a day. Sharks can survive for extended periods without feeding by storing energy in their liver as fats and oils. Amazingly, relatively inactive bottom-dwelling species, such as swellsharks, have survived in captivity for over a year without eating.

Feeding frenzies A common media image, and one that appears to confirm many people's prejudices regarding sharks, is the feeding frenzy—a pack of agitated sharks ripping into baits, and sometimes even each other. Such feeding frenzies, however, are actually rare in the wild and are usually the result of humans deliberately overloading the sharks' sensory systems by filling the water with blood and the odors of dead fishes. Then the normally well-ordered behavior of sharks breaks down. Competing for a limited amount of food, they swim rapidly in all directions, biting at anything that gets in their way.

ACTIVE AND PASSIVE
Above left: Though not active hunters, wobbegongs are nevertheless efficient predators that opportunistically take prey that happens into their vicinity. This ornate wobbegong makes a meal of a small Port Jackson shark.
Above: Sea lions are favored prey of some active sharks. A colony of sea lions, such as the one here, and fur seals around the Neptune Islands in South Australia draws the area's famous great white sharks.

87

DEFENSE STRATEGIES

Although other, larger sharks pose the main danger to sharks, they also fall victim to other predators. Sharks have a number of defense strategies to protect them from attack or to ward off would-be attackers. Some have inbuilt physical defenses such as dorsal fin spines or, as in the case of the swellshark, the capacity to swell their bodies by swallowing water.

Aggression Many of the larger, more active sharks use aggression as a form of defense. While this sometimes means that one shark will attack another, it is more common that a shark will first signal its aggressive intentions in order to avoid a physical attack. The best known aggressive (agonistic) display in sharks was first observed in gray reef sharks in the Marshall Islands.. Before attacking, the shark swam in an exaggerated fashion with its back arched and pectoral fins lowered. If the threatening object backed off, the shark would not attack. If the threat persisted, however, an attack was almost inevitable. Sharks may also display aggression by "tail cracking": swimming toward a threat, turning suddenly and flicking its tail with a loud crack.

WARNING SIGNS
The illustrations compare the threatening display of gray reef sharks (the top illustration in each view) with their normal non-threatening behavior (shown in the lower of each pair of illustrations). This posturing has been observed in response to other sharks and humans.

KEEPING OUT OF SIGHT

Camouflage is an effective form of
defense for many species of sharks. The
mottled coloration of angelsharks (right)
and wobbegongs makes them very difficult
to see as they rest in their reef habitat.
The weed-like tassels that surround the
mouth of the tasselled wobbegong (far
right) also aid in this camouflage.

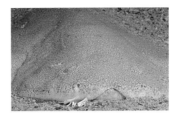

Camouflage Many benthic sharks
have striped, spotted or blotchy skin
patterns to provide camouflage. The
newborn young of some species, such
as tiger sharks, zebra sharks, gray
carpetsharks and whiskery sharks,
have vivid stripes or blotches that
eventually fade as they mature.
These markings provide maximum
camouflage when the sharks are
young and most vulnerable to
predation. Sharks that spend most,
or all, of their life swimming often
have coloration that reduces their
visibility in the water. In these
species, the underside is lightly
colored so that when viewed from
beneath the sharks blend with the
bright sunlit water. On the upper
side these sharks are darker so that
when viewed from above they are
difficult to distinguish from the
ocean around them.

SAFETY IN CAVES

Whitetip reef sharks often rest by day in
caves or under ledges which provide them
with maximum protection when they
would be most visible to predators, which
include other, larger sharks. At night these
sharks themselves become predators.

SOCIAL BEHAVIOR

While our knowledge of shark behavior is limited, it does appear that sharks spend much of their lives as solitary animals. For the most part they hunt, feed and live by themselves. We know that they do not form family groups and that there is rarely cooperation between individuals.

Sharks in groups While many sharks spend much of their time alone, some species are known to school. The purpose of these schools is subject to speculation as sharks, unlike smaller fishes, do not need to use them to avoid predation, nor do they feed when in schools. The best known schooling behavior is that of the scalloped hammerheads. In the Gulf of California, off the coast of Mexico, schools of up to 225 sharks have been seen, swimming around a sea mount during the day and dispersing at night to surrounding areas to feed. Similar schooling

COMING TOGETHER
Although sharks are solitary animals, they sometimes congregate, attracted by food or the need to reproduce or migrate, although data about this behavior is hard to gather. These Port Jackson sharks are in a mating group.

behavior has been observed in gray reef sharks in the Marshall Islands and in lemon sharks at the Bimini Islands in the Bahamas, although there are no more than 25 individuals in any one group. Other species, including piked dogfish, whiskery sharks, blacktip sharks and juvenile dusky sharks will occasionally congregate, but there is no coordination in their movements.

Pecking order Social interactions have been observed within schools or groups of sharks. While feeding on whale carcasses, large great white sharks will aggressively chase, or even severely bite, smaller great whites in order to assert their dominance within the species. Dominance hierarchies between species over food are also common, such as the interaction between

whitetip reef sharks (low dominance), gray reef sharks (middle dominance) and silvertips (high dominance). Similar hierarchies also exist for many species in non-feeding situations. For example, male bonnethead sharks will display a threat posture known as a "hunch" toward others in the group and will physically bump and bite females or smaller males. The most spectacular and well-documented example of social hierarchies in sharks is the agonistic (ready for combat) display of the gray reef shark, which was described on page 88. It is likely that within schools or aggregations other social interactions occur, but they have never been studied.

SOCIAL BEHAVIOR continued

Hammerhead sharks have a distinctive schooling behavior. When a number of these sharks swim together, each member of the school remains a set distance from its neighbor and all members move in the same direction.

Cooperative hunting While most sharks hunt alone, cooperative hunting has occasionally been observed. Sevengill sharks, for example, hunt in packs to capture large fur seals, which, at up to 775 pounds (350 kg), are more than twice the weight of the largest sevengill. By hunting as a group the pack of sharks can attack and consume an animal that a lone sevengill could never overpower. In the late 1980s Dave Ebert, of Rhodes University in South Africa, observed a group of sevengill sharks off the coast of Namibia. They first formed a loose circle around a fur seal. Then the sharks gradually moved inward, tightening the circle to prevent the seal from escaping. Eventually, one of the sharks attacked the seal. This was the signal for the other sharks to join the attack and start feeding. Cooperative hunting has not been studied in any other species of sharks. However, anecdotal evidence suggests that it may also occur in oceanic whitetips, thresher sharks, sand tigers and blacktip reef sharks.

Population segregation Shark populations are often organized so that animals of the same sex or size live in distinct parts of a species' range. In the waters off Trinidad, for example, adult female hammerheads occur in depths from 30 to 60 feet (9–18 m); adult males and large juveniles of both sexes occur in depths from 90 to 120 feet (27–36 m); and newborn pups live close to shore in depths of less than 30 feet (9 m). It is believed that population segregation may help reduce cannibalism, which could occur when sharks of different sizes interact, or may merely relate to different feeding preferences among the sharks of different age and sex. Whatever the reason, segregation of males and females breaks down during the mating season to allow for reproduction.

Courtship All species of sharks yet studied engage in some form of social reproductive behavior, because the male must copulate to fertilize the female's eggs. In many species, a male closely follows a female during the mating season with its nose near the female's vent. This is probably a way of informing chemical information about her reproductive condition. During courtship, a male may aggressively bite the back, flanks and fins of the female and may inflict severe wounds. Compared with other fishes, sharks produce a tiny number of offspring. To ensure that these offspring have the best possible chance of survival, females try to mate with only the healthiest, fittest males. To achieve this, sharks frequently undertake long pre-mating rituals. Competing male whitetip reef sharks become aggressive toward each other as they vie for the right to mate with a female. In the chain catshark, a small egg-laying species of the Atlantic, the pre-mating ritual lasts for more than an hour and includes biting and coordinated swimming.

SOLITARY SHARK
Our understanding of the social behavior of sharks is limited by incomplete research. The tasselled wobbegong, the most common tropical wobbegong, is frequently observed by divers. However, little is known of the social behavior of this solitary species, which seems only to congregate for mating purposes.

MATING AND REPRODUCTION

In stark contrast to most fishes, each mating of sharks produces a few well-developed young that have a high survival rate. Sharks provide nutrients and protection to their developing young in a number of ways: laying eggs; mammal-like placental nutrition; and even bizarre forms where unborn pups consume their siblings.

How sharks mate All male sharks have a pair of claspers between the pelvic fins on their underside. These claspers are short and soft in juveniles but become elongated and harden as the shark matures. During mating, a clasper is inserted into the female's cloaca and the sperm is transferred. While almost all observed matings have occurred on the sea floor, it is clear that the mating position of sharks varies with body form. In elongate, flexible species, such as the smallspotted catshark, the male wraps himself around the female's pelvic region. The males of less flexible species, such as the whitetip reef shark, position themselves alongside the female, holding one of her pectoral fins in their mouth to maintain the correct mating position. One clasper is inserted into the cloaca with the tip splayed outward to maintain its position. Some species, such as the piked dogfish, have

PROTECTING THE UNBORN
Port Jackson sharks lay their eggs in unique spiral egg cases. Newly hatched Port Jackson sharks are—except for their fins, which seem too large for their tiny bodies—perfect replicas of their parents.

spines and hooks on the end of the clasper for added anchorage. Mating can last from about 30 seconds in chain dogfish to 4 minutes in whitetip reef sharks.

Oviparity The simplest form of reproduction, observed in hornsharks, catsharks and epaulette sharks, is egg-laying. After fertilization, each egg is enclosed in a tough, flexible case. Some sharks lay a pair of eggs at a time, but may then go on to produce several dozen eggs from the same mating over an extended period. The egg cases are laid in protected areas or anchored to the ocean floor. The embryo's only source of nutrition is the large yolk within the egg. As it develops, a seam along one side of the egg case splits and water flows around the egg. To help the circulation of water, the developing shark swims within the case. When the yolk is exhausted it hatches through the open seam.

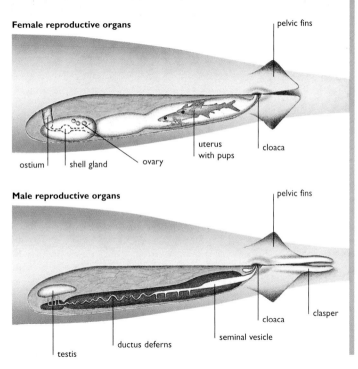

Female reproductive organs

pelvic fins
ostium — shell gland — ovary
uterus with pups
cloaca

Male reproductive organs

pelvic fins
testis
ductus deferns
seminal vesicle
cloaca
clasper

MATING AND REPRODUCTION continued

Ovoviviparity Only a small number of shark species have developed this reproductive method. It is similar to oviparity (egg laying) but provides greater protection to the developing embryos. The eggs, which are still encased, are retained within the female's body and never laid. The young hatch from the female's body and are born live.

Yolk-sac viviparity This is the most common reproductive method among sharks. The young are retained in the female's body and the yolk is the major source of nutrients for the developing embryos. However, the egg case is reduced to a thin membrane surrounding the embryo. In some species, such as the piked dogfish, this membrane contains a number of eggs. During development the yolk is stored in a thin-walled yolk sac, which is connected to the embryo by a thin cord. In addition to the yolk, some species may provide nutrients to the embryos by way of secretions from the uterus wall. Examples of species with yolk-sac viviparity include wobbegongs,

MATING BEHAVIOR
The reproductive organs of male sharks, or claspers, are the modified inner edges of the pelvic fins. They are used for the transferring of sperm to the female. During mating a single clasper is flared, rotated and inserted into the female's cloaca. The pictures at left show the claspers of the whale shark (far left) and the tasselled wobbegong (left).
Above: In a number of species "love bites," or mating scars can be seen on the females—tooth nicks, slashes and semicircular jaw impressions on the flanks, the back, pectoral fins and around the gill area. Biting by the male stimulates the female to copulate. This picture shows a mating bite wound on the gills of a female great white shark.

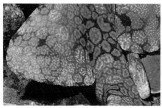

The tendrils on the egg case of the striped catshark anchor it to the reef or the bottom or, as here, to a convenient piece of kelp.

houndsharks, angelsharks and sevengill sharks.

Placental viviparity Some species have developed a system of embryonic nutrition similar to that of most mammals. Dusky, blue, hammerhead, spadenose, smooth-hound, blacktip and silvertip sharks develop a placenta and umbilical cord that provide a direct link between the mother and embryo for the exchange of nutrients, oxygen and waste. The placenta is usually

formed a couple of months into development of the embryos. To sustain the embryo prior to placental development, the eggs contain yolk, but much less than for egg-laying or yolk-sac-viviparous species. As the yolk is exhausted, the yolk sac fuses with the wall of the uterus to form the placenta. In the spadenose shark this system is so advanced that the eggs contain very little yolk and the placenta is formed within days.

Giving birth When they are ready to give birth female live-bearing sharks will often enter special nursery areas. These ensure that the young are safe from predation by

The age of many sharks can be determined by examining the number of concentric rings on their vertebrae. Most sharks produce one new ring each year.

larger sharks. Females stop feeding around the time of birth to further protect from predation. Prior to birth, they secrete a chemical that relaxes their uterus and eases the passage of the young. The pups emerge tail first and upside down, and are immediately able to swim. Pups' size varies enormously between species: the basking shark is believed to produce the longest young at around 66 inches (170 cm).

SPIRAL EGG CASES
The Port Jackson shark lays its eggs in distinctive dark-colored, spiral-shaped protective egg cases that are attached to the ocean floor or wedged into rocky crevices.

MIGRATION

Migration, either in groups or individually, is an important part of life for many species of sharks. Sharks migrate to find food and to reproduce, and in response to seasonal fluctuations in water temperature. Their migrations have been studied by releasing tagged sharks or by tracking individuals.

Why sharks migrate Sharks sometimes migrate to take advantage of food sources. For example, mako sharks move onto the continental shelf of the northeastern United States in summer to feed on schools of bluefish tuna that congregate there. Similarly, great white sharks migrate northward along the east and west coasts of Australia,

MOVING ALONG THE COAST
Tiger sharks, tagged off the east coast of the United States, have been shown to cover distances of more than 1,000 miles (1,600 km). These migrations are largely confined to the continental shelf.

following the migration of humpback whales to their summer pupping grounds. They feed on young whales that are sick or stray too far from their mothers. Sharks may also migrate to a mating area for reproduction. When it is time to pup, pregnant females may move to special nursery areas. Water temperature also plays a role in controlling migration routes. Many sharks have a preference for water of consistent year-round temperature. As water temperatures change with the seasons, these sharks migrate into waters of preferred temperature.

When sharks migrate Most sharks migrate annually. Each year during summer, for example, dusky, sandbar, blacktip and tiger sharks travel from the Gulf of Mexico to the east coast of the United States. Once there, they give birth before they

EPIC JOURNEYS
The map at left shows the migratory patterns of the blue shark (pictured at right) around the Atlantic Ocean, as revealed by an extensive tagging program. Individual sharks may travel incredible distances each year. The red lines indicate migration from tagging stations off the United States coast. The white lines show migration from other tagging stations.

migrate south again as winter approaches. They are replaced by dusky smoothhounds and piked dogfish that migrate from deep water to near the coast. In the waters around western Europe the piked dogfish population annually migrates through the North and Irish seas, and between Scotland and Norway. Other migrations are less regular.

Long-distance traveler The longest linear movement by an individual shark was recorded for a blue shark tagged off the coast of the northeast United States and recaptured 300 miles (500 km) south of the equator, a travel distance of 3,740 miles (6,000 km). Multiple recaptures of tagged blue sharks indicate regular transatlantic migrations over distances greater than 10,000 miles (16,000 km).

Daily movements In recent years scientists have used ultrasonic telemetry transmitters to record shark movements in their everyday environments. Studies of blue sharks off the coast of California show that individuals tend to spend daylight hours offshore and, after dark, move closer inshore to feed.

ELECTRONIC TAGGING
Most data about shark migration comes from long-term tagging programs, supported by government agencies, scientific researchers, and sport and commercial fishers. This great white shark has been fitted with an electronic tag.

PART TWO

KINDS OF SHARKS

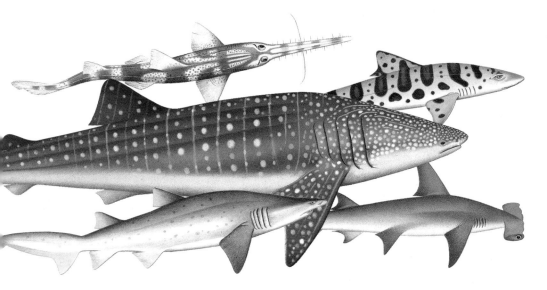

CLASSIFYING SHARKS

Classification and description of the 350 or so species of living sharks are based on the science of taxonomy, in which the morphological characteristics are used to group closely related species. Modern shark taxonomists use shared characteristics that have appeared in species throughout evolutionary history, such as the way the upper jaw is attached to the skull, how the skeletal structures are arranged and the shape of the teeth. Since such features cannot readily be observed in living animals, the keys we have for the identification of most organisms are still based largely on external features that can be observed or measured with relative ease.

SHARK ORDERS AND FAMILIES

While there is some disagreement among scientists regarding the classification of the 350 or so species of living sharks, they are generally divided into eight orders. These are further subdivided into 34 families, with a variable number of species in each. To identify shark species and classify them into orders and families, taxonomists rely on a fairly standard list of external features and measurements.

Frilled shark

Sixgill, sevengill and frilled sharks (order Hexanchiformes)

Comprising two families, these wide-ranging sharks have six or seven pairs of gill openings, instead of the usual five. They have an anal fin and a single, spineless dorsal fin.

Broadnose sevengill shark

Frilled sharks (family Chlamydoselachidae) have compressed, eel-like bodies. The mouth is at the tip of the snout rather than under the head, and they have teeth with three cusps in both jaws. There are one or two species.

Sixgill and sevengill sharks (family Hexanchidae) have cylindrical bodies, mouths under the head and large, comb-like teeth in the lower jaw. There are five described species.

Dogfish sharks (order Squaliformes)

The seven families in this order have two dorsal fins, no anal fin, a short to moderately long conical snout, and five pairs of gill openings. Most dogfish sharks occur in deep water on the slopes of continents and islands.

Bramble sharks (family Echinorhinidae) are large, cylindrical sharks with small, spineless dorsal fins over the pelvic fins. Their denticles are large and tack-like. There are two species.

Dogfish sharks (family Squalidae) are moderate-sized cylindrical sharks. They have compressed, single-cusped cutting teeth in both jaws and strong, ungrooved dorsal fin spines. There are 11 species.

Gulper sharks (family Centrophoridae) are moderate-sized cylindrical sharks with single-cusped cutting teeth in both jaws and broad dorsal fins with grooved spines. There are more than 14 species.

Lanternsharks (family Etmopteridae) are small to dwarf cylindrical sharks with grooved spines on the dorsal fins. They are named for their luminous organs. There are 45 species.

Sleeper sharks (family Somniosidae) are moderate-sized to

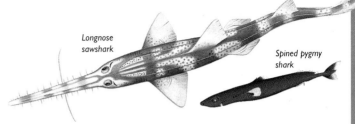

Longnose sawshark

Spined pygmy shark

gigantic cylindrical sharks with broad, moderate-sized dorsal fins and small hooked or flat denticles. There are more than 15 species.

Roughsharks (family Oxynotidae) have smallish, compressed bodies, giving them an inflated, triangular appearance. Their common name derives from the rough, hooked denticles on their skin. They have huge, broad dorsal fins with strong spines that are mostly buried within the fins. There are five or six species.

Kitefin sharks (family Dalatiidae) are dwarf to moderate-sized cylindrical, or slightly compressed sharks. They have broad dorsal fins. Some species have luminous organs.

There are at least nine species, including one of the world's smallest sharks, the spined pygmy shark.

Sawsharks
(order Pristiophoriformes)

There is one family (Pristiophoridae) of these small to moderate-sized, flat-headed sharks. Believed to be the closest living relatives of the rays, they have a long, saw-like snout with two long barbels. They also have two spineless dorsal fins, no anal fin and five to six pairs of gill openings. There are more than five species. They occur in shallow to deepish water on the shelves and slopes of the Indian, Pacific and North Atlantic oceans.

Prickly dogfish

Angelsharks (order Squatiniformes)

The angelsharks comprise a single family (Squatinidae) of moderate-sized, highly flattened sharks. While they resemble rays in appearance, they are only distantly related to rays. They have two small, spineless dorsal fins; no anal fin; a short, truncated snout with a mouth at the tip; five pairs of gill openings; and huge pectoral fins with angular extensions covering the gill openings. Most of the more than 15 species occur inshore in temperate waters. A few are found in deep tropical waters.

Bullhead sharks (order Heterodontiformes)

There is only one family (Heterodontidae) of these sharks. They are also known as hornsharks because of the spines on each of their dorsal fins. The heads of bullhead sharks are large in relation to their body size. They have five pairs of gill openings, two large dorsal fins and a short, pig-like snout. There are at least eight species, found in the warm continental waters of the Pacific and Indian oceans.

Carpetsharks (order Orectolobiformes)

This order comprises seven families that range in size from small to gigantic. They have two spineless dorsal fins, an anal fin, a short mouth in front of the eyes, five pairs of gill openings and nostrils with barbels. The pectoral fins of many species are specially adapted for "walking" on the ocean floor.

Collared carpetsharks (family Parascylliidae) are all small, narrow-headed, long-tailed and slender sharks. They have side grooves on the nostrils and a distinctive band surrounds the head, rather like a necklace. They have an angular anal fin, well in front of the short, low caudal fin.

Blind sharks (family Brachaeluridae), so named because they close their eyes when caught by anglers, are small, stocky, broad-headed, long-tailed sharks. They have side grooves on the nostrils and an angular anal fin that is slightly in

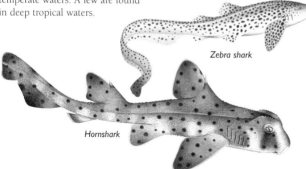

Zebra shark

Hornshark

front of the short, low caudal fin. There are two species.

Wobbegongs (family Orectolobidae) are small to large sharks. They have flat, broad bodies and short tails. They have conspicuous folds of skin on the sides of their heads; large, fang-like front teeth; and an angular anal fin that is slightly in front of the short, low caudal fin. Many of the six or more species are superbly camouflaged, most notably the tasselled wobbegong.

The 12 species—possibly more—of longtailed carpetsharks (family Hemiscylliidae) are divided into the epaulette and bamboosharks.

They are small, slender, narrow-headed sharks with a short, low caudal fin. Some species have ridges on the tail.

The single species of zebra shark (family Stegostomatidae) is large, stocky and broad-headed. It has a

tail that is almost as long as the rest of the body. There are no side grooves on the nostrils or keels on the tail, but there are prominent ridges on the body.

Nurse shark

Ornate wobbegong

Blind shark

The three species of nurse sharks (family Ginglymostomatidae) are small to large, and broad-headed. They have an angular anal fin just in front of the short, low caudal fin.

The single species of whale shark (family Rhincodontidae) is the largest living fish. This gigantic, broad-headed filter feeder has very large gill openings and internal filter screens. It has an angular anal fin well in front of the high, crescent-shaped caudal fin.

Mackerel sharks (order Lamniformes)

This order contains seven families of mostly large sharks. They have two spineless dorsal fins, an anal fin, five pairs of gill openings and a long mouth that extends past the eyes. Their eyes do not have nictitating eyelids and their nostrils lack barbels. They occur in almost all seas, predominantly in coastal and oceanic waters.

Goblin sharks (family Mitsukurinidae) are deepwater sharks with strange elongated, blade-like snouts. There is only one species of this large, soft-bodied shark.

Sand tiger sharks (family Odontaspididae) are large stout-bodied sharks with short snouts, narrow gill openings, large dorsal and anal fins and a short caudal fin with a small lower lobe. There are three or four species.

Crocodile sharks (family Pseudocarchariidae) are small, long, cylindrical sharks with short conical snouts, very large eyes, small fins and long, dagger-like teeth. There is only one species.

The single species of megamouth shark (family Megachasmidae), only discovered in 1976, is a very large deepwater filter feeder. Its huge mouth is at the end of its very short, broadly rounded snout.

Thresher sharks (family Alopiidae) are large, stout-bodied sharks with large pectoral fins, big eyes and an enormous caudal fin. There are three or four species.

Basking sharks (family Cetorhinidae) are gigantic, stocky filter feeders with enormous gill openings, a conical snout and a short, crescent-shaped caudal fin.

Bronze whaler

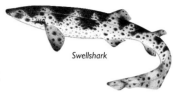

Swellshark

They are the second largest living fish. There is only one species.

Mackerel sharks (family Lamnidae) are large to very large, spindle-shaped sharks with very broad gill openings and a short, crescent-shaped caudal fin. There are five species.

Ground sharks (order Carcharhiniformes)

Sharks in the eight families of ground sharks range from small to very large. They have two spineless dorsal fins, an anal fin, a short mouth in front of the eyes, five pairs of gill openings and nostrils that usually lack barbels. These sharks are dominant in terms of abundance and number of species.

Catsharks (family Scyliorhinidae) are small, slender sharks with the

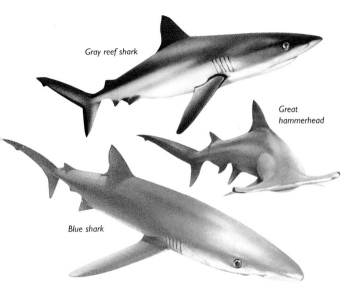

Gray reef shark

Great hammerhead

Blue shark

and comb-like teeth at the mouth corners. There are at least two species of false catsharks.

Barbeled houndsharks (family Leptochariidae) are small sharks with barbels on the nostrils, an arched mouth and long labial furrows. There is only one species.

Houndsharks (family Triakidae) are small to fairly large. They have an arched or angular mouth and generally no barbels on the nostrils. There are more than 36 species.

The more than seven species of weasel sharks (family Hemigaleidae) are small to fairly large, slender sharks. Their eyes are nearly circular.

Requiem sharks (family Carcharhinidae) range from small to very large. They have nearly circular eyes and precaudal pits. There are more than 50 species.

Hammerhead sharks (family Sphyrnidae) are small to very large. They are similar to requiem sharks except for their "hammer" heads. There are at least eight species.

first dorsal fin over or behind the pelvic fin. This largest of shark families has 104 species.

Finback catsharks (family Proscylliidae) are small, slender sharks. They have angular mouths with comb-like teeth at the corners. There are at least five species.

False catsharks (family Pseudotriakidae) are small to large sharks. They have deep grooves in front of their eyes, an angular mouth

NAMING SHARKS

Many species of sharks are widely known by several common names, or are called different common names in different parts of the world. Clearly this can lead to confusion. It can even mean that two people are talking about the same shark and are not aware of it. Often some of these common names are based on widely held assumptions, and frequently misconceptions, about their nature and behavior.

Great white shark

Judging by appearances

Carcharias taurus—the sand tiger, according to the International Commission on Zoological Nomenclature—is known as the gray nurse in Australia. In North America and New Zealand it is referred to as the sand tiger; in South Africa it is the spotted raggedtooth shark.

Brown catshark

The variety of names given to this species seems to stem from its appearance and from media coverage of shark attacks. It is fierce-looking, and its long, protruding teeth and yellow eyes are easy to associate with danger and terror. In fact, as shark experts have noted, it is relatively inoffensive and not aggressive unless provoked. It seems that reputedly dangerous sharks attract the greatest number of common names. *Carcharodon carcharias,* the great white shark, is also known as the white pointer, the white shark, the

great blue shark or even, melodramatically, as the white death. The shortfin mako, *Isurus oxyrinchus,* is sometimes called the blue pointer, a name that causes confusion with both the blue shark, *Prionace glauca,* and the great white—or blue—shark.

Scientific names

The value of internationally recognized scientific names is to remove much of this confusion. Taxonomy refers to the classification of organisms within related groups of various sizes. However, even scientific names are not set in concrete. New discoveries keep the classification of all organisms in a state of flux.

SHARK CLASSIFICATION
This diagram summarizes much of the material in the previous pages. It shows the main similarities and differences between each of the eight major groups, or orders, of sharks.

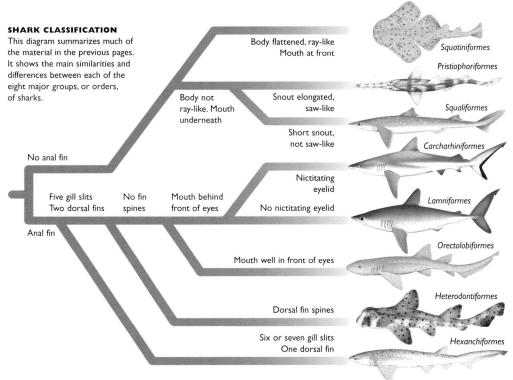

Body flattened, ray-like
Mouth at front

Squatiniformes

Pristiophoriformes

Body not ray-like. Mouth underneath

Snout elongated, saw-like

Squaliformes

Short snout, not saw-like

Carcharhiniformes

No anal fin

Five gill slits
Two dorsal fins

No fin spines

Mouth behind front of eyes

Nictitating eyelid

No nictitating eyelid

Lamniformes

Anal fin

Mouth well in front of eyes

Orectolobiformes

Dorsal fin spines

Heterodontiformes

Six or seven gill slits
One dorsal fin

Hexanchiformes

HEXANCHIFORMES

Hexanchiformes are sharks that have a single spineless dorsal fin, six or seven pairs of gill openings—most sharks have only five—and an anal fin. This small group contains two families—frilled sharks (family Chlamydoselachidae), and sixgill and sevengill sharks (family Hexanchidae). There are five described species and perhaps another two yet to be positively identified. These sharks are worldwide in their distribution and occur mostly in deepwater locations. Members of this group are ovoviviparous live-bearers—the young hatch from eggs within the female's body.

FRILLED SHARK

The frilled shark is often referred to as a living fossil because of its close resemblance to the early sharks of the Paleozoic era. While some experts think it is a direct descendant of the primitive ancient Cladoselache sharks; others maintain that it is descended from more modern forms. Although it usually lives at considerable to great depths, it is occasionally observed at or near the surface.

Appearance The frilled shark has an unmistakable elongate, eel-like body, which is medium to dark brown. It has one dorsal fin and six pairs of gill slits, each with frilled margins. The first of the frills almost encircles the head, giving the appearance of a collar. The mouth is just below the short snout and contains approximately 300 small, widely spaced tricuspid teeth. The eyes are large.

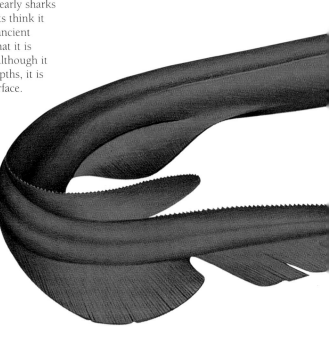

♂ ♀ 6 ½ ft (2 m)

Other names
Frill-gilled shark, eel shark
Size at birth 16 in (40 cm)
Maximum length 6 ½ ft (2 m)
Diet Other sharks, squid and fishes
Habitat Benthic, on the continental slopes and island margins, usually at depths of 400–4,200 ft (120–1,280 m)
Distribution Wide-ranging but patchy in all oceans except northwestern Atlantic coast

Chlamydoselachus anguineus

Reproduction The frilled shark is ovoviviparous and, after a gestation period lasting one to two years, gives birth to between eight and 15 pups per litter.

Comment The frilled shark is a rare, peculiar and poorly understood deepwater shark.

BLUNTNOSE SIXGILL SHARK

This massive, powerful shark is one of four species with six pairs of gill slits. The sixgill sawshark, frilled shark and bigeye sixgill shark are the others. It uses its long tail to swim in a strong, constant motion. It is a common species, which is most often seen at night all year round. The bluntnose sixgill is a voracious predator of other large fishes. The little we know of its biology has been gleaned mainly from data from commercial fisheries. It is widely fished for both its meat and its oil.

Appearance This shark is large and stout-bodied, with a small dorsal fin at the back of the body, slightly in front of an even smaller anal fin situated below. It has a long tail, a broad head and a broadly rounded snout. Its large comb-like teeth are arranged in rows, and its small fluorescent green eyes are set wide apart. It is usually pale to dark gray or chocolate brown on the upper body and its underside is grayish white. Some members of the species, however, are blackish both above and below. The coloring is generally paler along the lateral line.

Reproduction Little is known about this species, except that it is ovoviviparous. It produces between 22 and 108 pups per litter.

Comment Although it may attack if provoked, the bluntnose sixgill shark is not generally considered dangerous to humans.

KEY FACTS

♂♀ 15¾ ft (4.8 m)

Other names
Sixgill shark, bull shark
Size at birth 24–28 in (60–70 cm)
Maximum length 15¾ ft (4.8 m)
Diet Wide-ranging, including other sharks, rays, bottom fishes and even crabs and seals
Habitat Shelves and slopes from the surface to 6,500 feet (2,000 m)
Distribution Coastal, worldwide including oceanic islands

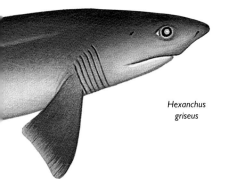

Hexanchus griseus

BROADNOSE SEVENGILL SHARK

This shark is immediately recognizable because of its seven pairs of gill slits—most shark species have only five pairs. Although the species is widespread, it is not particularly abundant. It will often come close inshore in shallow bays and inlets, but does not rest on the seabed. This may explain why it is not commonly seen by divers. There are no records of it attacking people (except for divers in aquariums), but it will scavenge on human corpses. It is, however, potentially dangerous and should be treated with due caution.

Appearance One of only two species of shark that has seven pairs of gills (the other being the sharpnose sevengill shark), the broadnose sevengill shark has a large, heavy, tapering body with a long tail. It has one small dorsal fin. It has a broad head and a blunt snout and its eyes are small. The teeth of the broadnose sevengill are very effective for cutting. Those in the upper jaw are—except for a

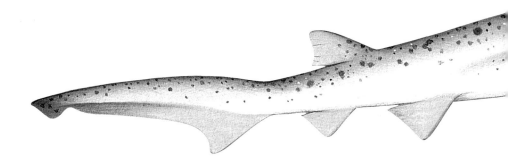

single middle tooth—jagged with cusps; the teeth in the lower jaw are sharp and comb-like. The upper part of the body is a silvery gray to brown color and is speckled with distinctive dark gray or black spots. The underside is pale. Juveniles have white margins on their rear fins. The teeth of the broadnose sevengill are very effective for cutting.

Reproduction The broadnose sevengill shark is ovoviviparous, bearing live young in shallow bays. Litter sizes vary, and can be as large as 82 pups. Females breed in spring and summer.

Comment This species is quite common off South Africa and Namibia.

KEY FACTS

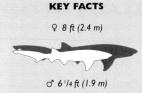

♀ 8 ft (2.4 m)

♂ 6 ¼ ft (1.9 m)

Other names
Cow shark, groundshark
Size at birth 16–18 in (40–45 cm)
Maximum length 10 ft (3 m)
Diet Wide-ranging, including other sharks, rays, bottom fishes and seals
Habitat Shallow bays and estuaries along the continental shelf to 450 feet (135 m)
Distribution Temperate coastal shelves, except for northern Atlantic

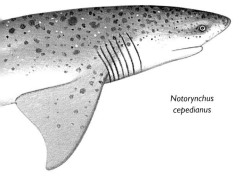

Notorynchus cepedianus

SQUALIFORMES

The squaliformes, or dogfish sharks, are a large and varied group that contains seven families and comprises at least 94 species. They are found in all oceans at depths up to 20,000 feet (6,000 m). Most occur in deep water on the slopes of continents and islands, but some inhabit temperate inshore waters, and a few range as far as the Arctic and Antarctic regions. All have two dorsal fins (either spined or spineless), no anal fin, cylindrical bodies, short to moderate snouts and five pairs of gill openings. Many have powerful cutting teeth in both jaws.

BRAMBLE SHARK

The bramble shark is one of only two sharks in the family Echinorhinidae. The other is the prickly shark *Echinorhinus cookei*, found in the Pacific, from the Americas to Hawaii, New Zealand and Asia. The bramble shark takes its name from its large and very prominent spine-like denticles, which are about half an inch (12 mm) in diameter at their base. They are scattered over the shark's body and on the underside of the snout in adults and are sometimes fused into plates. This fairly common and widespread species is most frequently encountered in the Mediterranean Sea and along the west coasts of Europe and Africa.

Appearance This sluggish deepwater shark has a stout, cylindrical body with two dorsal fins and a thick caudal fin. The anal fin is absent. The dorsal fins, which have no spines, are of similar size and are located at the back of the body, close to the pelvic and caudal fins. The first dorsal fin is directly over the pelvic fins. The bramble shark has relatively large, oval-shaped eyes, a

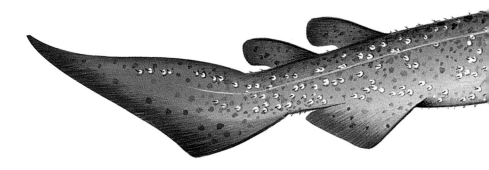

short snout and small spiracles. Its head is slightly flattened. The skin is a dark purplish gray to brown, often with darker spots on the back and sides. The underside is lighter in color. Large, spiny, plate-like denticles are irregularly scattered over the body. The mouth is broadly arched and the lips are smooth.

Reproduction This species is ovoviviparous, bearing litters of between 15 and 26 young.

Comment Although usually slow-moving, the bramble shark is capable of surprising speed in short bursts.

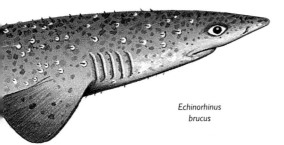

Echinorhinus brucus

KEY FACTS

♀ 7¼ ft (2.2 m)

♂ 5¼ ft (1.6 m)

Other names Spinous shark
Size at birth 1–3 ft (30–90 cm)
Maximum length 10 ft (3 m)
Diet Smaller sharks, fishes and crabs
Habitat Continental shelves and upper slopes, from 1,300 to 3,000 ft (400–900 m)
Distribution Western Atlantic from Massachusetts to Virginia; Argentina; eastern Atlantic from North Sea to Mediterranean and southern Africa; India; New Zealand; southern Australia; Japan

PIKED DOGFISH

The piked dogfish, commonly known also as the spiny dogfish, is possibly the world's most abundant shark and, because of its commercial importance, supports a fishing industry of global significance. However, its slow growth rate and low rate of reproduction make it highly vulnerable to overharvesting. In some areas this has resulted in the near depletion of its stocks. These sharks form extremely large schools, routinely frequenting the shallow and coastal waters of higher latitudes in spring and fall, and migrating into deep waters during the cooler winter months.

Appearance The piked dogfish has a slender cylindrical body. It has two dorsal fins, with spines that are mildly poisonous. Like all the Squaliformes, it lacks an anal fin. The pectoral, pelvic and caudal fins have pale posterior margins. There are two dorsal fins, set wide apart. The first, which is larger than the second, is situated in front of the pelvic fins. A long, pointed snout and sharp, blade-like teeth also

typify this species. Piked dogfishes range in color from bluish, through gray, to brown. The upper body and flanks are often covered with white spots that fade as the shark grows older. The underside is lighter. This shark has prominent eyes. The large spiracle being each eye is an identifying feature of this widespread and fairly common species.

Reproduction The piked dogfish is ovoviviparous. After a gestation period of 18–24 months, females give birth to up to 20 live young. This gestation period is the longest known for any shark.

Comment Piked dogfish have a long life expectancy. A life span of 70 years is not uncommon.

KEY FACTS

♀ 3¼ ft (100 cm)

♂ 2½ ft (80 cm)

Other names Spiny dogfish, skittledog, white-spotted dogfish, spotted spiny dogfish, spurdog, Victorian spotted dogfish, codshark, thornshark
Size at birth 8–12 in (20–30 cm)
Maximum length 5 ft (1.5 m)
Diet Small fishes, krill and squid
Habitat Coastal, from very shallow water to 2,600 ft (800 m)
Distribution Atlantic and Pacific oceans; southwest Australia; tip of Africa

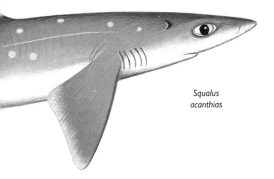

Squalus acanthias

SMALLFIN GULPER DOGFISH

One of 14 members of the family Centrophoridae, known collectively as gulper dogfishes, the smallfin gulper dogfish is a common deepwater shark in some parts of its range. However, its numbers have been significantly depleted in recent years as a result of overharvesting. Although this small shark, which measures barely 3 feet (1 m) in length, looks less impressive than the very large sharks often caught by big-game fishers, it is economically of much greater importance. Along with numerous other species of dogfish sharks, it is much sought after.

Appearance This slender, elegant deepwater shark has two dorsal fins with grooved spines (the second fin is small) and elongated pectoral fins with pointed rear tips. As in all Squaliformes, the anal fin is absent. It has blade-like teeth in both jaws; a long, narrow snout; and large, green eyes. It is light gray to gray-brown on the upper body and fins, and its underside is white. The tips of the dorsal fin and the upper lobe of the caudal fin are marked with dusky or black patches. The young often have a pair of arrow-like barbs on the dorsal fin spines.

Reproduction The smallfin gulper dogfish is ovoviviparous. In summer females give birth to litters of two pups. The gestation period is at least one year, but can in some cases be as long as two years.

Comment The flesh of the smallfin gulper dogfish is firm, tasty and nutritious. It is widely fished and is used in Mediterranean and South American cuisines.

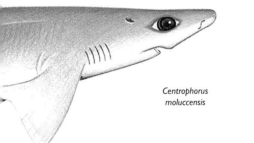

Centrophorus moluccensis

KEY FACTS

♀ 39 in (98 cm)

♂ 34 in (86 cm)

Other names Endeavor dogfish, arrowspine dogfish
Size at birth 12–15 in (30–38 cm)
Maximum length 39 in (98 cm)
Diet Pelagic and bottom fishes, small dogfish sharks, squid, octopus, shrimp and tunicates
Habitat Benthic, on the outer continental shelves and upper slopes at depths of 420–2,700 ft (130–820 m)
Distribution Indo-West Pacific; scattered records from eastern South Africa eastward to Australia and Japan

BLACKBELLY LANTERNSHARK

Lanternsharks, members of the family Etmopteridae, are the most numerous of the Squaliformes. Their name comes from the bioluminescent organs that run along their underside. These organs provide an effective form of camouflage by enabling the sharks to blend in with the weak illumination that filters down from the surface. The sharks produce just enough light to equal the amount of down-welling light between them and the ocean's surface. Because of this optical illusion, they merge with the ocean and cannot be seen by potential predators—or by unsuspecting prey.

Appearance A small and slender shark, the blackbelly lanternshark has two spined dorsal fins (the rear one being about twice the size of the first) and no anal fin. Its eyes, spiracles and nostrils are all large, and the snout is short. The upper body is light brown, merging to darker brown on the flanks and nearly black on the lower body.

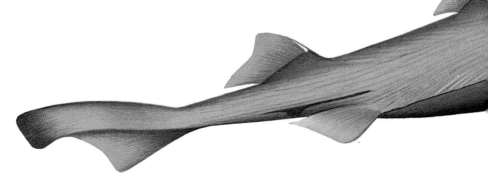

Black markings are present on the underside. The sharp, blade-like teeth are well adapted for its diet of fishes and cephalopods. A number of features distinguish the blackbelly lanternshark from other lanternsharks. Among them are the number and arrangement of its denticles and slight differences in fin size and color.

Reproduction It is presumed that, like other Squaliformes, the blackbelly lanternshark is ovoviviparous, but little is known of its reproductive biology or the size of the litter.

Comment The blackbelly is closely related to the dwarf lanternshark *Etmopterus perryi*, which at 8 inches (20 cm) long is probably the smallest living shark.

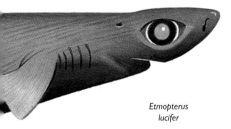

Etmopterus lucifer

KEY FACTS

♂ 13 ³/₄ in (35 cm)

♀ 13 ¹/₂ in (34 cm)

Other names Lucifer shark
Size at birth 6 in (15 cm)
Maximum length 18 in (45 cm)
Diet Squid, shrimp and small fishes
Habitat Along slopes and shelves at depths of 590–3,300 ft (180–1,000 m)
Distribution Southern and eastern Australia; New Zealand; China Sea to Japan (Records from southern Africa and South America are possibly not this species)

GREENLAND SLEEPER SHARK

This shark, the only polar shark of the Atlantic, is a real deepwater dweller that lives in near-freezing conditions at depths of up to 1,800 feet (550 m). It rises to more shallow water only in the colder months. At such depths and temperatures, it will not be encountered by divers, although it has been caught by fishers. It is a sluggish beast—sleeper is an appropriate name—and provides little resistance when captured. Nevertheless, because of its size, it should be handled carefully in captivity.

Appearance This gigantic dogfish is almost cylindrical. It has two small, spineless dorsal fins and an asymmetrical caudal fin. As with other sleeper sharks, the anal fin is absent. The Greenland sleeper shark has a short, rounded snout, green eyes and relatively large spiracles. It is grayish pink in color, with darker bluish black fins. The teeth of the upper jaw are long and pointed, while those on the lower jaw are oblique, sharp and closely set. These teeth allow the Greenland sleeper shark to gouge large chunks of flesh from dead cetaceans, and probably to remove the heads of seals and sea lions before eating the carcasses.

Reproduction This species is ovoviviparous, bearing approximately 10 pups, each 15 inches (38 cm) long, per litter.

Comment The Greenland sleeper shark lives in water temperatures of 36–45°F (2–7°C). Despite its huge size, it is not dangerous to humans.

KEY FACTS

♀ 12 ft (3.7 m)

♂ 9 ½ ft (2.9 m)

Other names
Sleeper shark, gurry shark
Size at birth 15 in (38 cm)
Maximum length 21 ft (6.4 m)
Diet Seals, bottom fishes, invertebrates and carrion
Habitat From shallow water to 1,800 ft (550 m)
Distribution North Atlantic Ocean

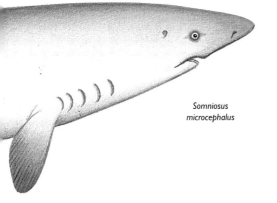

Somniosus microcephalus

PRICKLY DOGFISH

The prickly dogfish is one of only four species of
roughsharks, members of the family Oxynotidae.
It is one of the most unusual looking sharks of the
deep ocean bottom. Its most distinctive physical
features are the high, spined dorsal fins with their
forward extensions, which give the appearance
of sails.

Appearance This shark's stout body is laterally triangular in shape. It has a flattish head, prominent spiracles, large eyes and a small, fleshy, slot-like mouth. Its skin is covered in small, prickly denticles. There are two large, spined dorsal fins and no anal fin. There is a visible ridge on the abdomen.

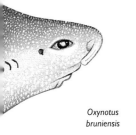

*Oxynotus
bruniensis*

Reproduction The prickly dogfish is ovoviviparous. Females give birth to litters of about seven pups. Very little else is known of its biology.

Comment Although the prickly dogfish is common around parts of the southern Australian and the New Zealand coasts, this dweller of the ocean deeps is rarely sighted and has not been extensively studied. Its range is restricted mainly to temperate coastal waters, but it is occasionally found in tropical regions off the coast of Queensland, Australia.

KEY FACTS

♀ 2²/₅ ft (73 cm)

♂ 2 ft (60 cm)

Other names None
Size at birth 4 in (10 cm)
Maximum length 2½ ft (73 cm)
Diet Bottom invertebrates
Habitat Temperate waters, from 165 to 1,640 ft (50–500 m)
Distribution Southern Australia and New Zealand

COOKIECUTTER SHARK

This is one of three species in the genus *Isistius*, the others being the China Sea cookiecutter, *I. labialis*, and the largetooth cookiecutter, *I. plutodus*. Before its feeding behavior was discovered, this species was known as the cigar shark because of its long, thin, brown body. The more recent name arises from its distinctive teeth, jaws and lips, which enable the cookiecutter to form a suction cap with its lips on the skin of its prey, bite and then swivel around to cut out a neat circular or oval plug of tissue—just like a cookiecutter in pastry.

Appearance This chocolate-colored, cigar-shaped shark has two small dorsal fins toward the rear of its body, a nearly symmetrical caudal fin and no anal fin. It has a distinctive dark collar around the gill slits. Its head is notable for large eyes with green pupils, short conical snout and fleshy, suctorial jaws and lips. The enlarged, razor-sharp,

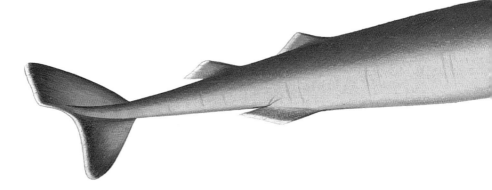

saw-like triangular teeth enable the cookiecutter shark to grasp bites of flesh from its prey, leaving a distinctive scar. The shark's victims include marlins, tunas, seals, whales and dolphins. It has even damaged the rubber coating of underwater cables in US Navy hydrophones and the rubber dome of a nuclear submarine.

Reproduction Like other Squaliformes, the cookiecutter is ovoviviparous. Little is known of its reproductive biology or litter size.

Comment The cookiecutter can turn a luminous green. This is possibly a way of attracting and ambushing prey.

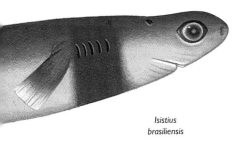

Isistius brasiliensis

KEY FACTS

♀ 20 in (50 cm)

♂ 16 in (40 cm)

Other names
Cigar shark, luminous shark
Size at birth Unknown
Maximum length 20 in (50 cm)
Diet Squid, and pieces of large fishes and marine animals
Habitat Oceanic, migrating from depths of 3,300 ft (1,000 m) to the surface each night
Distribution Widespread, mostly oceanic

SPINED PYGMY SHARK

This tiny but widespread shark lives in the cold depths of temperate and tropical waters, offshore near continental and island landmasses. Like other deepwater sharks, it makes a daily migration to feed. It rises at dusk, stopping within 650 feet (200 m) of the surface, and feeds during the night on squid, shrimp and midwater fishes. Lanternfishes are a particular favorite of this species. The bioluminescent photophores on its underside camouflage the spined pygmy shark from predators as it feeds. With the coming of dawn, it descends once again to the depths.

Appearance This tiny shark has a spindle-shaped body, with two asymmetrical dorsal fins (the first being significantly smaller than the second), small rounded pectoral fins and an almost symmetrical caudal fin. It has no anal fin. The first dorsal fin is the only one to carry the spine that gives this shark its common name. Its eyes and spiracles are large, and the snout is bulbous and pointed. It is unusual in color, being dark brown to jet black, with lighter fin margins. The ventral surface is bioluminescent, which helps the shark to blend in with the weak illumination from the water surface when viewed from below.

Reproduction This species is probably ovoviviparous but, as with many Squaliformes, little is known of its reproductive biology or litter size.

Comment The spined pygmy rivals the dwarf lanternshark *Etmopterus perryi* as the world's smallest shark.

KEY FACTS

♀ 8 in (20 cm)

♂ 7 in (18 cm)

Other names Dwarf shark, midwater shark
Size at birth less than ¹/₂ in (12 mm)
Maximum length 10 in (25 cm)
Diet Squid, shrimp and midwater fishes
Habitat Offshore, at depths of 650–6,500 ft (200–2,000 m)
Distribution All oceans

Squaliolus laticaudus

PRISTIOPHORIFORMES, SQUATINIFORMES, HETERODONTIFORMES

Each of these three orders consists of a single family. Pristiophoriformes—the sawsharks—are a minor group of harmless bottom-dwelling sharks that resemble small swordfishes. There are five species of these. The ray-like angelsharks, or Squatiniformes, are distinguished by their flattened bodies and mottled surface. There are at least 15 species of these sharks. Bullhead sharks, or Heterodontiformes, are unique in having spines on their two dorsal fins and an anal fin. There are eight described species of Heterodontiformes.

LONGNOSE SAWSHARK

Although sawsharks are widely distributed in the Atlantic, Pacific and Indian oceans, this common species is confined to the temperate waters along the coasts of southern Australia. Divers may come across this shark lying on the sandy bottom. It is a timid and generally harmless species, but may lash out with its powerful snout if handled. It feeds by trailing its barbels along the sea bottom to locate small bony fish. The teeth on the snout then stir up sediment to rouse the prey.

Appearance The longnose sawshark is a medium-sized shark with a slender, elongate body, large pectoral fins and two dorsal fins. It does not have an anal fin. The head is depressed and the long, flattened snout, which can comprise up to 30 percent of the shark's length, resembles a saw, with slender, needle-like teeth on the edges and two barbels midway, in front of the

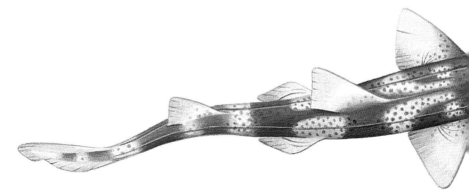

nostrils. The longnose sawshark is sandy to grayish brown in color with irregular brown splotches scattered on the skin. The underside is pale. The skin is covered with tiny denticles, which give it a soft feel, and the dorsal and pectoral fins are scaly to the touch.

Reproduction This species is ovoviviparous. It breeds in winter and the female produces between three and 22 pups per litter. The pups are born with the teeth of the saw folded back against the blade to avoid injury to the mother during birth.

Comment This shark, like others in its family, is often confused with the sawfish, which is an elongate ray.

*Pristiophorus
cirratus*

PACIFIC ANGELSHARK

The alternative common name of the angelshark is
monkshark or monkfish. These names originated
from the strange shape of this shark's head which
was thought to resemble the hood of a monk's cloak.
The Pacific angelshark spends its day buried in sand,
with only its eyes and head exposed. In this position
it is ready to burst forth and seize hold of an
unsuspecting fish or squid in its protruding jaws and
spiky teeth. It was once a common species but its
numbers have been considerably reduced in recent
times as a result of heavy fishing.

*Squatina
californica*

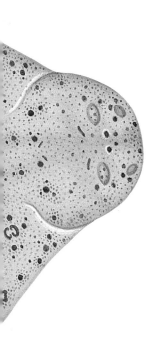

Appearance This shark is flattened, with the edges of the pectoral fins free from the body. The pectoral and pelvic fins are broad with rounded tips, while the dorsal, anal and caudal fins are quite small. It has a blunt nose and large spiracles. The eyes are on the top of the head and the gill slits are on the underside of the body. A sluggish shark, it is camouflaged by its speckled sandy gray or brown color. The underside is white.

Reproduction This species is ovoviviparous. Females give birth to about 8–13 pups per litter; the larger the female, the larger the litter.

Comment Although this species is not considered to be dangerous to humans, it will bite if it is attacked or provoked.

KEY FACTS

♀ 5 ft (150 cm)

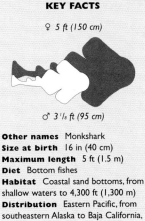

♂ 3 1/8 ft (95 cm)

Other names Monkshark
Size at birth 16 in (40 cm)
Maximum length 5 ft (1.5 m)
Diet Bottom fishes
Habitat Coastal sand bottoms, from shallow waters to 4,300 ft (1,300 m)
Distribution Eastern Pacific, from southeastern Alaska to Baja California, and from Ecuador to southern Chile

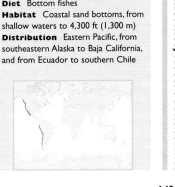

Pristiophoriformes, Squatiniformes, Heterodontiformes

HORNSHARK

The hornshark is named for the spine in front of each of its dorsal fins. It is one of at least eight species in the family Heterodontidae, which consists of the six hornsharks, as well as the bullhead and Port Jackson sharks. The scientific name of the genus, *Heterodontus* (from Greek for "mixed-tooth"), refers to the small pointed teeth at the front of these sharks' jaws and the blunt teeth at the rear. With these versatile teeth, they are well equipped to grasp a variety of other sea creatures on which they prey.

Appearance This rather odd-looking, sluggish shark has two spined dorsal fins and an anal fin. It uses its large pectoral fins to "walk" along the ocean floor. Its enlarged head has prominent ridges over the large eyes and a pig-like snout. The skin is sandy to gray in color with darker spots. It is rough in texture. The underside is yellowish white.

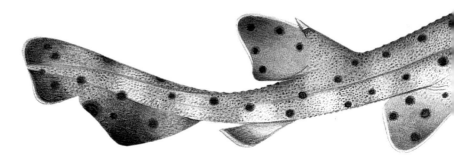

Reproduction This is an oviparous shark. A female lays two eggs a month for three months of the year. She then carries the corkscrew-shaped egg cases in her mouth before wedging them into crevices for protection.

Comment This sedentary species, popular in aquariums, defies the belief that all sharks must swim in order to breathe. It spends most of its day lying placidly on the seafloor.

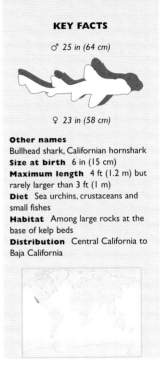

KEY FACTS

♂ 25 in (64 cm)

♀ 23 in (58 cm)

Other names
Bullhead shark, Californian hornshark
Size at birth 6 in (15 cm)
Maximum length 4 ft (1.2 m) but rarely larger than 3 ft (1 m)
Diet Sea urchins, crustaceans and small fishes
Habitat Among large rocks at the base of kelp beds
Distribution Central California to Baja California

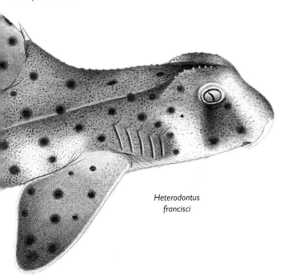

Heterodontus francisci

145

ORECTOLOBIFORMES

Orectolobiformes are popularly known as carpetsharks. All the members of this small but diverse group of seven families and at least 37 species of warm-water sharks have pig-like snouts and short mouths that in most cases are connected to the nostrils by grooves. They have an anal fin but they differ from the bullhead sharks in having no fin spines on the two dorsal fins. Carpetsharks have uniquely formed barbels at the inside edges of the nostrils. They are all sharks of warm temperate or tropical waters in shallow to moderate depths. They are found largely in the tropics of the western Pacific and the Indian oceans.

NECKLACE CARPETSHARK

This is one of six described collared carpetsharks in two genera, *Parascyllium* and *Cirrhoscyllium*. The necklace carpetshark, which is found only in southern Australian waters, is active at night, when it is sometimes encountered by divers. During the day it is difficult to spot because it rests in caves or on the sandy bottom, where it is perfectly camouflaged by its cryptic patterning.

Appearance Rather eel-like in appearance, the necklace carpetshark has a slender, tubular, elongate body. Its two dorsal fins are of similar size. It also has an anal fin and a long caudal fin. The head and snout are slightly depressed, the eyes are oval and set well behind the mouth, and

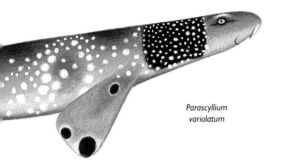

Parascyllium variolatum

♂ ♀ *3 ft (90 cm)*

Other names Varied carpetshark, southern carpetshark, varied catshark
Size at birth Unknown
Maximum length 3 ft (90 cm)
Diet Unknown, however the dentition would suggest benthic crustaceans
Habitat Continental shelves to 1,600 ft (500 m)
Distribution Southwestern Australia to southern Australia

the spiracles are small. Two short barbels hang from the underside of the snout. This shark is fawn, with brown and white spots all over the body. A wide, dark collar, speckled with white spots, encircles the neck around the gills, and black saddles adorn the fin margins.

Reproduction This species is oviparous, but little else is known about its reproductive biology.

Comment This harmless shark has been little studied and information about it is limited.

BLIND SHARK

Despite its common name, this harmless species is not blind, but appears to be so as it rotates its eyeballs backward when frightened, such as when it is taken from the water. It is one of only two species in the blind shark family, the other being the bluegray carpetshark *Heteroscyllium colcloughi*. Although often referred to as catsharks, these sharks are related only distantly to the true catsharks. The blind shark is nocturnal, sheltering under ledges and in caves during the day and emerging at night to forage on the reef and in the sand.

Appearance The blind shark has a stout, cylindrical, brown body with paler spots. Its two spineless dorsal fins, which are of similar size, are close together, with the first originating above the pelvic fins. The smooth skin is covered with small denticles. It has very large spiracles behind and to the side of the eyes. The nostrils are well developed, with a pair of long, smooth barbels connected to the

mouth by a groove that permits water that has passed over the olfactory organs to flow into the mouth. The small groove in the middle of the chin distinguishes the blind shark from its relative, the bluegray carpetshark. The young have prominent, dusky cross-bands that disappear as the shark ages.

Reproduction The blind shark is ovoviviparous, giving birth to seven or eight pups per litter in late spring or summer.

Comment This shark can live in very shallow water, just deep enough to cover it. It also inhabits the deeper waters of the continental shelf.

KEY FACTS

♂♀ 4 ft (1.2 m)

Other names Brown catshark
Size at birth 7 in (18 cm)
Maximum length 4 ft (1.2 m)
Diet Reef fish and invertebrates
Habitat Rocky shores from tide pools to 330 ft (100 m)
Distribution Central eastern Australia

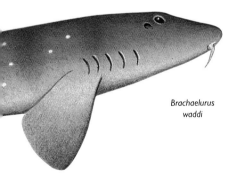

Brachaelurus waddi

ORNATE WOBBEGONG

The ornate wobbegong, like the other five members of its family, is a master of camouflage. A common inshore inhabitant of temperate rocky and tropical reefs, it rests during the day, usually in the open on rocky bottoms or table coral, where it is perfectly camouflaged by its cryptic markings. It becomes active at night, searching the reef for invertebrates and fishes. Twenty-three provoked and unprovoked attacks have been documented in Australian waters from careless encounters with divers and fishers.

*Orectolobus
ornatus*

Appearance This ornately patterned nocturnal wobbegong has two similar-sized dorsal fins on the rear part of its body, an anal fin, and broad pectoral and pelvic fins. Its flattened body tapers from behind the pelvic fins. It has five or six narrow flaps of skin on each side of the head, two nasal barbels, sharp teeth and large spiracles. It is brown with light and dark marbling, with darker saddles and paler patches. There is a white spot behind each spiracle. It is pale on the underside.

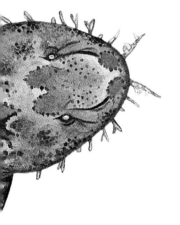

Reproduction Like all wobbegongs, the ornate wobbegong is ovoviviparous, giving birth to at least 12, but usually 20 or more, pups per litter.

Comment Although seemingly harmless, wobbegongs can inflict a nasty bite when accidentally disturbed by divers and fishers.

KEY FACTS

♂♀ 9½ ft (2.9 m)

Other names Banded wobbegong, carpetshark, gulf wobbegong
Size at birth 8 in (20 cm)
Maximum length 9½ ft (2.9 m)
Diet Bottom invertebrates and bony fishes
Habitat Inshore, from shallow water to 330 ft (100 m)
Distribution Papua New Guinea; eastern, southern and southwestern Australia

EPAULETTE SHARK

The epaulette shark is one of 12 described species of longtailed carpetshark, members of the family Hemiscylliidae. There are two genera—the epaulette sharks, *Hemiscyllium*, and the bamboosharks, *Chiloscyllium*. Most of these sharks are small, with thin, slightly flattened, elongate bodies. The epaulette shark is reasonably common within its range. Divers often encounter adults resting during the day, but juveniles are rarely seen, as they take refuge within the coral or rocky reefs, which are their principal habitats.

Hemiscyllium ocellatum

Appearance The epaulette shark has a slender body with two dorsal fins of similar size and an anal fin set well back. It has a rounded snout, two short nasal barbels and large spiracles. It is colored for camouflage, and is golden or tan

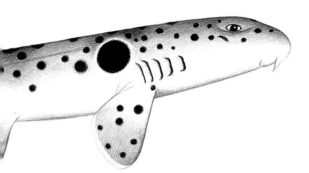

KEY FACTS

♂♀ 3 ¹/₂ ft (107 cm)

Other names
Ocellated bambooshark
Size at birth 6 in (15 cm)
Maximum length 3 ¹/₂ ft (107 cm)
Diet Benthic invertebrates
Habitat Shallow inshore reefs
Distribution New Guinea;
northwest to northeastern Australia

with large, widely spaced black spots. Juveniles have colored bands above the pectoral fins. These change to a prominent black spot as the shark matures. This distinctive feature is surrounded by a thick white ring.

Reproduction This is an oviparous species. The female lays two eggs at night in brown cases about 4 inches (10 cm) long. The eggs hatch in about 130 days.

Comment The epaulette shark is well suited to captivity in aquariums. Females in aquariums have been known to lay 50 fertile eggs per year.

ZEBRA SHARK

Also popularly known as the leopard shark because of the brown spots on an adult's yellowish body, this beautiful shark is widespread among the coral reefs of the tropical Pacific and Indian oceans. It is a sluggish species. Divers occasionally encounter one resting on the bottom during the day, propped up on its pectoral fins, facing into the current with its mouth open in order to obtain oxygen more easily from the water.

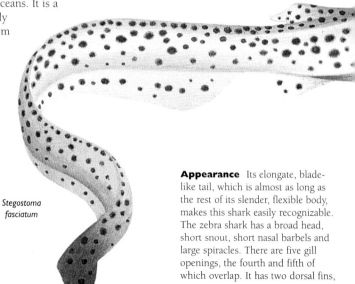

Stegostoma fasciatum

Appearance Its elongate, blade-like tail, which is almost as long as the rest of its slender, flexible body, makes this shark easily recognizable. The zebra shark has a broad head, short snout, short nasal barbels and large spiracles. There are five gill openings, the fourth and fifth of which overlap. It has two dorsal fins,

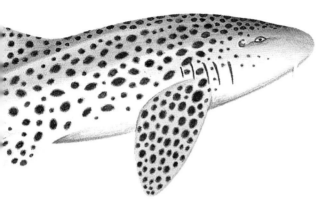

KEY FACTS

♂♀ 6 ¹/₂ ft (2 m)

Other names
Leopard shark, blind shark
Size at birth 8 in (20 cm)
Maximum length 11 ¹/₂ ft (3.5 m)
Diet Mollusks, crustaceans and
bony fishes
Habitat Shallow water; common
in coral reefs
Distribution Tropical western
Pacific and Indian oceans to eastern
Africa

which are set close together. There is
an anal fin and the pectoral fins are
large and rounded. Prominent ridges
run along the upper part of the body.
Adults are yellowish to brown with a
pale underside. The shark gets its
common name from the coloring of
the juveniles, which have yellow
stripes on a black background.

Reproduction This species is
oviparous. Females lay eggs in large
brown or black cases, which are
covered with hairy tufts. These help
hold the eggs firmly on the seabed
until they hatch.

Comment The zebra shark moves
sluggishly and poses no danger to
humans.

Nurse Shark

No one is sure how this shark got its common name—perhaps from the suckling noise made by a feeding nurse shark, which sounds like a nursing baby. Common over inshore coral reefs in tropical waters, the nurse shark is sluggish during the day, but active at night, when it feeds on bottom-dwelling invertebrates and other fish. It is aggressive to humans only when provoked. Because they are abundant, easy to capture and adapt well to captivity, nurse sharks are commonly seen in public aquariums and oceanariums. Behaviorists have used them extensively to study learning in sharks.

Appearance This fairly large, sluggish, nocturnal bottom-dweller has a broad head and a fairly stout body. Nasal grooves run between the nostrils and the corners of the small mouth, and noticeable barbels protrude from the nasal openings. There is a small spiracle behind and below each eye. The nurse shark has large, rounded dorsal and pectoral fins, an anal fin and a relatively long caudal fin. The color is yellowish brown or tan to dark brown. The lower body is a lighter color. There is no pattern, except on juveniles, which have dark spots and obscure saddles which fade with age.

Reproduction Nurse sharks are ovoviviparous. A female gives birth to between 20 and 28 pups in a litter.

Comment These are probably the most common sharks seen by snorkelers and divers in the Caribbean. They are often observed resting quietly on the ocean floor.

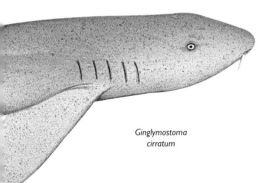

Ginglymostoma cirratum

KEY FACTS

♀ 8 ¼ ft (2.5 m)

♂ 8 ft (2.4 m)

Other names None
Size at birth 11–12 in (27–30 cm)
Maximum length 14 ft (4.3 m), but rarely larger than 10 ft (3 m)
Diet Benthic crustaceans, shellfish, octopus, squid, and very slow fishes
Habitat Shallow inshore reefs and mangrove flats to 40 ft (12 m)
Distribution Western Atlantic from Rhode Island to Brazil; eastern Atlantic; eastern Pacific from Mexico to Peru

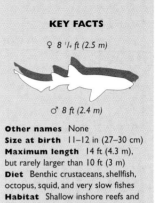

WHALE SHARK

The sole surviving member of its family, Rhincodontidae, the whale shark is the world's largest living fish. This filter feeder swims slowly near the surface, consuming its prey, which can include fish as large as mackerel. It frequently enters tropical lagoons, where it mixes contentedly with snorkelers and divers.

Appearance This huge and very distinctive shark has a stout body, a broad, flat head and a truncated snout. It has 300 rows of tiny teeth in each of its jaws. There are two dorsal fins (the second being significantly smaller than the first),

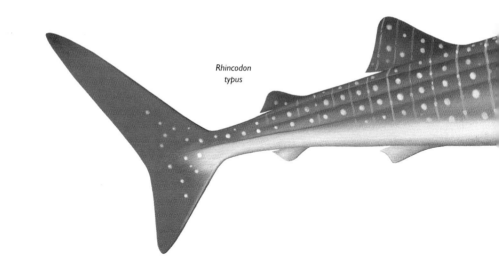

Rhincodon typus

an anal fin, lateral ridges on the trunk and tail and a crescent-shaped caudal fin with a long lower lobe. Its coloring is either gray, blue or brown and its underside is white. Light spots and vertical and horizontal lines create a checkerboard pattern.

Reproduction Until recently whale sharks were thought to lay eggs. They are now known to be ovoviviparous, producing huge litters of up to 300 young.

Comment Despite its size, the whale shark is harmless to humans unless captured or harassed. It is hunted in some parts of its range.

KEY FACTS

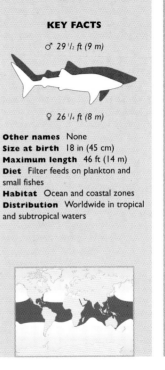

♂ 29 ½ ft (9 m)

♀ 26 ¼ ft (8 m)

Other names None
Size at birth 18 in (45 cm)
Maximum length 46 ft (14 m)
Diet Filter feeds on plankton and small fishes
Habitat Ocean and coastal zones
Distribution Worldwide in tropical and subtropical waters

LAMNIFORMES

Lamniformes, known as mackerel sharks, comprise seven families and 15 or 16 species. They are found right throughout the world, except in the coldest seas. They range from the intertidal to depths of more than 4,000 feet (1,200 m), and from the surf line to the great ocean basins. Most mackerel sharks have elongated snouts, long mouths, an anal fin and two spineless dorsal fins. These ovoviviparous sharks share with some others a form of uterine cannibalism: before birth, embryo sharks feed on their younger siblings and fertilized eggs.

GOBLIN SHARK

Until it was rediscovered in the 1890s, it was assumed that the goblin shark, a sluggish bottom-dweller on continental shelves and outer slopes, had been extinct for 100 million years. It was known only from early specimens that had been preserved through the ages. Even today, very little is understood about this deepwater shark, which is the sole member of its family, Mitsukurinidae.

Appearance Often described as the ugliest and most bizarre of living sharks, the goblin shark is recognizable by its long dagger-like snout, flattened in the shape of a paddle, which extends far in front of

*Mitsukurina
owstoni*

its mouth. Its jaws, which protrude prominently when extended, contain large, slender, needle-like teeth at the front—ideal for grasping small fish—and small teeth at the back, which form a crushing or binding plate for processing captured prey. This shark has a flabby body which is pinkish gray, becoming slightly darker in the gill area and on the fins. It has two dorsal fins and an anal fin. Its eyes are tiny.

Reproduction The species is thought to be ovoviviparous, but little is known so far about its biology or the size of its litter.

Comment Living in the ocean depths, goblin sharks are rarely seen. Occasionally, however, one is spotted in shallow water near the shore.

KEY FACTS

♂♀ 9 ¹⁄₂ ft (2.9 m)

Other names Elfin shark
Size at birth Unknown
Maximum length 12 ³⁄₄ ft (3.9 m)
Diet Little is known. However, its fragile, pointed teeth indicate soft-bodied prey such as pelagic squid and shrimp
Habitat Upper continental slope, near the bottom, at 1,180–1,800 ft (360-550 m)
Distribution Scattered tropical and temperate locations in the Atlantic, Indian and Pacific oceans

SAND TIGER

The sand tiger is one of four species, known collectively as sand tiger sharks, that belong to the family Odontaspididae. Like its relatives, it is a large, fearsome-looking, but essentially gentle, shark that swims slowly with its mouth open, exposing its long, narrow, needle-like teeth to view. A feature of the sand tiger shark is its ability to hover motionless in the water. It does this by swallowing surface air and holding it in its stomach, thus achieving near-neutral buoyancy. It is also known to make long coastal migrations for reproductive purposes. It lives mainly in shallow bays and sandy coastal waters and on rocky or tropical reefs.

Appearance The sand tiger has a bulky, stout body. Its two large dorsal fins, roughly equal in size, are also about the same size as the anal fin. The asymmetrical caudal fin has a long upper lobe. There is a precaudal pit but no caudal keels. This shark has small, light-colored eyes, a short, pointed, flattened snout, protrusible jaws, a long mouth and long, narrow, needle-like teeth. Its gill openings are short. The upper body is lightish brown or sandy-colored and the underside is paler. Juveniles have small yellow or brownish spots that fade as the shark grows older.

Reproduction The sand tiger is ovoviviparous. In each of two uterine chambers, the first embryo to hatch devours the other developing siblings. Two live young are born after a gestation period of eight to nine months.

Comment Unless provoked, it is not dangerous to humans.

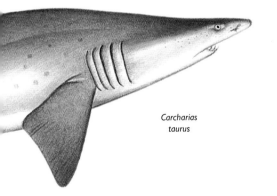

Carcharias taurus

KEY FACTS

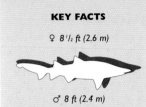

♀ 8½ ft (2.6 m)

♂ 8 ft (2.4 m)

Other names Gray nurse, sand shark, (spotted) raggedtooth shark
Size at birth 3¼ ft (1 m)
Maximum length 10½ ft (3.2 m)
Diet Fishes, rays, crabs and lobsters
Habitat Coastal, from sandy beaches and reefs to 625 ft (190 m)
Distribution Northwestern and eastern Atlantic; Gulf of Mexico; Argentina; southern Africa; Red Sea; Australia; Indonesia; China Sea to Sea of Japan

CROCODILE SHARK

The only member of the family Pseudocarchariidae, the crocodile shark is a relative of the sand tiger. This muscular and highly streamlined shark is widespread throughout the open oceans in tropical and subtropical regions and is also sometimes seen offshore. It is probably a fast-swimming predator that chases small prey, either near the surface or down to the 1,000 feet (300 m) mesopelagic zone. It is thought to be active mainly at night. With its powerful jaws and long, thin, sharp teeth—which are similar in shape to those of the larger mako sharks—the crocodile shark is very well equipped to seize hold of its small midwater prey. However, it is not dangerous to humans.

Appearance Named for its long, narrow-cusped, dagger-like teeth, the crocodile shark has a long, spindle-shaped body with two dorsal fins (the first being significantly larger than the second), an anal fin and rounded pectoral fins. Its caudal fin is short and asymmetrical with a moderately long ventral lobe and there are precaudal pits and low, lateral caudal keels. It has a long, conical, pointed snout, protrusible jaws and fairly long gill openings. One of its most distinctive features are the huge eyes, which have no nictitating membranes. The body is gray to dark brown above and grades to a paler shade on the underside. There are often dark blotches scattered over the sides and bottom surface. The fin margins are white.

Reproduction The species is ovoviviparous, giving birth to four pups per litter. In each of two uterine chambers two unborn pups survive after eating their sibling embryos. They continue to develop by feeding on eggs produced by the mother.

Comment Little is known of the crocodile shark's biology or lifestyle.

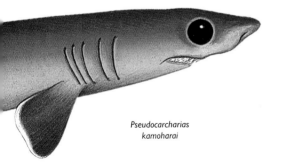

Pseudocarcharias kamoharai

KEY FACTS

♀ 3 ¹/₈ ft (95 cm)

♂ 3 ft (90 cm)

Other names None
Size at birth 16 in (40 cm)
Maximum length 3 ¹/₄ ft (1 m)
Diet Probably small fishes, squid and crustaceans
Habitat Mainly oceanic, probably midwater, from the surface to 1,900 ft (590 m)
Distribution All tropical and subtropical areas

THRESHER SHARK

This shark is one of three thresher sharks of the family Alopiidae. It is widespread in tropical and temperate waters and, although it often lives at considerable depths, it is commonly observed swimming at the surface in coastal waters. It is best viewed from boats or by snorkelers in open water. It frightens its prey and herds it into tight groups by slapping the water surface with its large, strong tail. It also uses its tail to stun prey. The thresher shark has been targeted by fisheries for its fins and meat and numbers, especially in many coastal areas, have decreased significantly as a result of overfishing.

Appearance The thresher shark has a husky, spindle-shaped body with large pelvic fins, two dorsal fins—although the second of these is minute—a tiny anal fin and broad, curved pectoral fins with pointed tips. It has a short, conical snout; large eyes—without nictitating membranes—placed well forward on the head; relatively small jaws filled with rows of remarkably efficient small, sharp teeth; and fairly short gill slits. There are prominent labial furrows at the sides of the jaws. The most distinctive feature of the

Alopias vulpinus

thresher shark is the long upper lobe of the caudal fin, which is equal in length to the rest of the body. The body is pale to dark blue-gray above, with a sharp, ragged line marking the edge of the underside, which is pale gray or white.

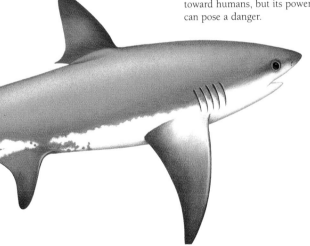

Reproduction This species in ovoviviparous and oophagous—unborn pups consume unfertilized eggs released by the mother. A female gives birth to a litter of two to four pups after a gestation period estimated at nine months.

Comment It is not aggressive toward humans, but its powerful tail can pose a danger.

KEY FACTS

♀ 15 ft (4.6 m)

♂ 11 ¾ ft (3.6 m)

Other names Fox shark, whiptail shark, thintail thresher shark
Size at birth 4–5 ft (1.2–1.5 m)
Maximum length 18 ft (5.5 m)
Diet Small schooling fishes
Habitat Coastal and oceanic, from the surface to 1,200 ft (365 m)
Distribution Cosmopolitan in temperate and tropical seas

MEGAMOUTH SHARK

The aptly named megamouth shark was not known until 1976, when a large, black, blubbery shark was accidentally captured off Hawaii. The creature had become entangled in a deepwater net line. Certain of its characteristics suggested a relationship with the ecologically disparate white sharks and makos. A new genus, species and family was created, known as the megamouth shark. Its scientific name comes from the Greek to mean "giant yawner of the open sea." Since this shark was discovered, barely a dozen other megamouth sharks—including three females—have been observed.

Appearance As its common name suggests, the megamouth shark has an enormous mouth; it extends behind the eyes, measures more than 40 inches (1 m) in width and contains over 100 rows of tiny teeth. This mouth may be luminous, enabling the shark to attract plankton. The megamouth's body is large, flabby and cylindrical, with two dorsal fins, (the first much larger than the second); an anal fin; long, narrow pectoral fins; and an asymmetrical caudal fin with a long upper lobe. Coloring is dark brown or gray to black, lighter on the flanks to pale on the underside. The fins have white margins.

Reproduction Nothing is known of the reproductive biology or litter numbers of this species.

Comment Some of the specimens that have been observed have been washed alive onto beaches.

KEY FACTS

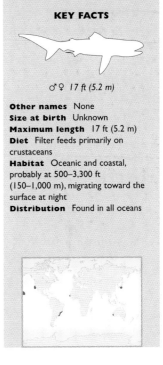

♂ ♀ 17 ft (5.2 m)

Other names None
Size at birth Unknown
Maximum length 17 ft (5.2 m)
Diet Filter feeds primarily on crustaceans
Habitat Oceanic and coastal, probably at 500–3,300 ft (150–1,000 m), migrating toward the surface at night
Distribution Found in all oceans

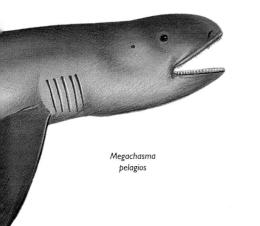

*Megachasma
pelagios*

BASKING SHARK

Among sharks the basking shark is second in size only to the whale shark and is therefore the world's second largest fish. Its huge size alone makes it easy to identify. This shark frequently visits temperate waters, where it takes advantage of seasonal plankton blooms in coastal regions. It often enters large bays to feed and can be seen close to shore, swimming slowly near the surface with mouth open wide to form a huge "net." Water passes into the mouth and across the gill rakers, which strain out the plankton before the water emerges through the gill slits.

Appearance The huge basking shark has a stocky body, with two dorsal fins (the second being significantly smaller than the first), an anal fin, a crescent-shaped caudal fin and lateral keels. Its broad gill slits extend around the top and bottom of the head. The short, pointed snout is narrow and conical, with huge jaws that expand laterally when the shark feeds on its preferred diet of plankton and crustaceans. The basking shark is a filter feeder; its hooked teeth are therefore

Cetorhinus maximus

minute, while the gill arches, which strain plankton from the surrounding water, are impressively large. Its coloring ranges from dark blue, through brown, to charcoal and gray. The underside is paler.

Reproduction Little is known of the basking shark's reproductive biology, as no pregnant females have been observed. However, it is thought that this species is ovoviviparous and oophagous—unborn pups consume unfertilized eggs released by the mother.

Comment This species is occasionally killed for its oil (squalene), fins, skin and meat. Although it is generally harmless, its huge size can make it dangerous when threatened or provoked.

KEY FACTS

♀ 29 ¼ ft (8.9 m)

♂ 21 ½ ft (6.5 m)

Other names Bone shark, elephant shark, sailfish shark
Size at birth 5–6 ½ ft (1.5–2 m) (est.)
Maximum length 49 ¼ ft (15 m), but few exceed 33 ft (10 m)
Diet Filter feeds on plankton and small crustaceans
Habitat Coastal, usually near surface
Distribution Most temperate seas, but only in small parts of Indian Ocean

GREAT WHITE SHARK

A star of film and literature, the great white is the most feared of sharks. It has been deemed responsible for the majority of unprovoked attacks on humans. Despite this, increasing numbers of sport divers descend in protective steel cages to observe this superb predator at close quarters. It prefers shallow, cool, coastal waters, but is occasionally seen as close to the equator as Hawaii. It hunts during the day for its varied prey, which includes other sharks and marine mammals.

Carcharodon carcharias

Appearance The great white shark has a stout, torpedo-shaped body, with two dorsal fins; long, narrow pectoral fins; a crescent-shaped caudal fin; and an anal fin. The second dorsal and anal fins are both small. It has large gill slits, a conical snout and black eyes. The serrated, triangular teeth are razor-sharp. Unlike those of its relatives, its teeth in the top and bottom jaws are almost symmetrical. The upper body varies in color from slate brown, through charcoal, to blue-gray, while the lower body is white or cream.

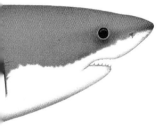

Reproduction The great white is viviparous and oophagous—unborn pups consume unfertilized eggs released by the mother. There are seven to nine pups in a litter.

Comment Fishing is seriously depleting stocks of this shark, which is easily caught as it hunts around coastal colonies of breeding seals. The species is now protected in South Africa, the Maldives, Namibia, Israel and several states of the United States and Australia.

KEY FACTS

♂♀ 11 ¹/₅ ft (3.4 m)

Other names White shark, white death, white pointer, blue pointer
Size at birth 3–4 ft (90–120 cm)
Maximum length reports of 24 ft (7.3 m)
Diet Seals, sea lions, dolphins, porpoises, sharks, carrion, seabirds, turtles, bony fishes and invertebrates
Habitat Coastal cooler waters with seal colonies, extending to tropics and open ocean
Distribution Worldwide in temperate seas; also Hawaii (rarely)

SHORTFIN MAKO

Ernest Hemingway's novel *The Old Man and the Sea*, published in 1952, reinforced the shortfin mako's reputation as a fighting sport fish. This widely distributed and fastest moving of all the sharks uses its speed to bear down on and capture its prey. It is also a long-distance swimmer. One individual was tracked traveling 1,332 miles (2,128 km) in 37 days, an average of 36 miles (58 km) a day.

Isurus oxyrinchus

Appearance The streamlined body of the shortfin mako is almost perfectly suited to traveling at high speed through the water. It has two dorsal fins, the second of which is much smaller than the first; narrow pectoral fins; a crescent-shaped caudal fin; and a tiny anal fin. The conical snout is quite pointed, the gill slits are long and the eyes are large and dark. The long, curved, dagger-like teeth are visible even when the shark's mouth is closed. The color of the shortfin mako is distinctive: metallic indigo blue on top, with a white underside.

Reproduction This species is ovoviviparous but lacks a placental connection. Litters of four to 16 pups are common. These sharks are also oophagous—unborn pups consume unfertilized eggs released by the mother.

Comment Sport fishers seek out the shortfin mako, not only for its tasty flesh, but also for the challenge it presents. It is capable of spectacular leaps—20 feet (6 m) in the air—and of bursts of speed of more than 22 miles per hour (35 km/h), when hooked.

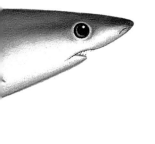

KEY FACTS

♀ 11 ft (3.4 m)

♂ 8 ft (2.4 m)

Other names Blue pointer, mackerel shark, snapper shark, mako shark, bonito shark
Size at birth 2–2½ ft (60–70 cm)
Maximum length 13 ft (4 m)
Diet Bony fishes, sharks, squid and oceanic whales and dolphins
Habitat Coastal and oceanic, from the surface to 500 ft (150 m)
Distribution All temperate and tropical seas

PORBEAGLE SHARK

This shark is extremely powerful and fast. It shares
with its North Pacific relative, the salmon shark, the
generic name *Lamna*. To the ancient Greeks, *lamna*
signified "a horrible monster of man-eating
tendencies," and it was invoked to frighten naughty
children. The salmon and porbeagle sharks resemble
each other so closely that they were not recognized
as separate species until 1947.

*Lamna
nasus*

Appearance The porbeagle has a stocky body, a minute second dorsal and anal fin and a crescent-shaped caudal fin. It and the salmon shark are the only species to have a secondary keel at the base of the caudal fin. This efficiently cuts the

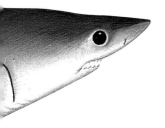

water in the shark's side-to-side swimming movement. This shark has a conical snout, large deep green eyes and sharp, slender teeth. The upper body is grayish blue to charcoal and the underside is white. There is a white spot at the base of the first dorsal fin.

Reproduction This species is ovoviviparous but lacks a placental connection. Litters are of one to five pups. These sharks are also oophagous—unborn pups consume unfertilized eggs that are released by the mother.

Comment One of the smallest of the five mackerel sharks, the porbeagle is often mistaken for the shortfin mako. It has suffered dramatically from overfishing, particularly in the North Atlantic.

KEY FACTS

♂ 8¼ ft (2.5 m)

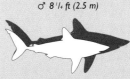

♀ 7 ft (2.1 m)

Other names Mackerel shark
Size at birth 2½ ft (75 cm)
Maximum length 10 ft (3 m)
Diet Bony fishes, other sharks and squid
Habitat Inshore and oceanic, from the surface to 1,200 ft (370 m)
Distribution Most temperate seas except North Pacific

CARCHARHINIFORMES

Carcharhiniformes, or ground sharks, dominate the world's shark fauna. The eight families contain 215 described species, as well as other species yet to be described. They are very widespread, living in cold to tropical seas, as well as in fresh water. The species are varied in a gradient from primitive small, inactive, small-toothed catsharks, through the intermediate houndsharks and weasel sharks, to the large, powerful requiem sharks and hammerheads, which predominate in warm seas. Most of the potentially dangerous species occur in this group.

BROWN CATSHARK

Although the brown catshark is quite a common dweller in the cold waters along the west coast of North America, little is known about its lifestyle. It is one of the 106 known species of catsharks—so named because their eyes resemble those of cats—and one of the 31 so far identified members of the genus *Apristurus*. Like most members of this genus, brown catsharks seem to be fairly sluggish and sedentary and to move only short distances during their entire lives. Unlike many other *Apristurus* species, this medium-sized catshark, though a deepwater shark, does not live on the ocean bottom.

Appearance Like most catsharks, the brown catshark has a large head, slender, tapering body and weak, thin tail. It is a body structure that is suited to the pronounced eel-like motion that characterizes their swimming, with the motive force provided by the whole rear end of the body—and not just the tail. It has two dorsal fins of similar size,

*Apristurus
brunneus*

set far back, small pectoral fins and a long anal fin that stretches to the start of the elongate caudal fin. The eyes are small with nictitating membranes. This harmless species has small teeth, relatively large gill slits and a long, broad snout. As its name suggests, it is chocolate brown on the upper body and underside, with pale fin margins.

Reproduction This shark is oviparous. A female lays one egg at a time in a case 2 inches (5 cm) long. It is believed that the eggs hatch after about 12 months.

Comment Attempts have been made to keep and study brown catsharks, and other *Apristurus* species, in captivity, but these have so far proved unsuccessful.

KEY FACTS

♂ 21 in (53 cm)

♀ 18 in (45 cm)

Other names None
Size at birth 3 in (7.5 cm)
Maximum length 2¼ ft (68 cm)
Diet Pelagic shrimp, squid and small fishes
Habitat Continental shelves and slopes from 100 to 3,000 ft (30–900 m), well above the bottom
Distribution British Columbia to Baja California

SWELLSHARK

One of the largest catsharks, the sluggish, nocturnal, and highly distinctive swellshark is impossible to mistake for any other shark. But divers, and other fishes, frequently overlook these well-camouflaged dwellers among the rocks and kelp forests on the seabed. Swellsharks get their common name from their habit of swallowing water when threatened. In this way they can balloon themselves up to three times their normal size—until they become wedged tightly inside a rock crevice or other narrow hiding place and are safe from predators.

*Cephaloscyllium
ventriosum*

Appearance This shark has a broadly rounded snout, two small dorsal fins on the rear half of its stout body, an anal fin and a long caudal fin. The body is covered in large, spiky denticles. Its camouflage is provided by the patterning of dark

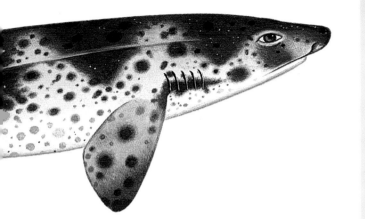

KEY FACTS

♂♀ 2³/₄ ft (83 cm)

Other names None
Size at birth 5¹/₂ in (14 cm)
Maximum length 3¹/₂ ft (1 m)
Diet Bottom fishes
Habitat Beneath and around kelp beds associated with reefs from depths of 30–200 ft (10–60m)
Distribution Temperate eastern Pacific, from California to Mexico and central Chile

brown blotches and saddle-like patterns on the yellow to brown background of its back as well as by the small dark spots on its underside and flanks. It has a huge, grinning mouth with small, pointed teeth that help it capture its prey of crustaceans and fish. Juvenile swellsharks are lighter in color than adults; they get darker as they grow older.

Reproduction The species is oviparous, laying two eggs at a time in greenish amber, purse-shaped cases among seaweeds. These hatch after seven to 10 months, depending on the temperature of the water.

Comment Swellsharks are not dangerous to humans unless they are handled or provoked.

187

GRACEFUL CATSHARK

The graceful catshark is one of about five species of finback catsharks, members of the family Proscylliidae. Finback catsharks are similar to true catsharks (members of the family Scyliorhinidae), but differ in having the first dorsal fin in front of or above the pelvic fins. In true catsharks it is behind them. The graceful catshark, alone among the finbacks, is oviparous. The others are ovoviviparous live-bearers. This shark is found above island and continental shelves in warm temperate and tropical waters.

Proscyllium habereri

Appearance This bottom-dwelling species has a slender body with two spineless dorsal fins of equal size, an anal fin, rounded pectoral fins and a long caudal fin. Like other finbacks, it has no precaudal pit and no strong ventral caudal lobe. It has a long snout and large, elongate, cat-like

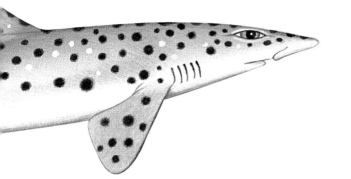

♀ 20 in (50 cm)

♂ 16 ½ in (42 cm)

Other names None
Size at birth Unknown
Maximum length 26 in (65 cm)
Diet Bony fishes and crabs
Habitat Continental shelves at depths of 165–330 ft (50–100 m)
Distribution Western Indo-Pacific, from southern Japan to Indonesia

eyes with nictitating membranes. There is a prominent spiracle behind each eye; this is used for ventilation. The mouth extends well beyond the eyes and the teeth are extremely small. The labial furrows in the corner of the mouth are small or absent and there are no nasal barbels. The graceful catshark is tan, and large and small dark spots cover the whole of the body.

Reproduction The species is oviparous. It is thought that females lay one egg per uterine chamber. Little else is know about its reproductive biology.

Comment The graceful catshark is harmless to humans. It is not common within its range and is rarely seen by divers.

FALSE CATSHARK

The false catshark is a large, fairly widespread, slope-dwelling shark that lives mainly in cold waters. However, it has an uneven distribution that extends its range into some tropical waters. It is one of only two described false catsharks, members of the family Pseudotriakidae. The other is the much smaller slender smoothhound, *Gollum attenuatus*. There is also an as yet undescribed dwarf species. The false catshark's body is watery and soft, which may help to give it the neutral buoyancy that suits its somewhat sedentary lifestyle on or near the bottom. Females of this species are thought to reach sexual maturity when just over 7 feet (2.1 m) long.

Pseudotriakis microdon

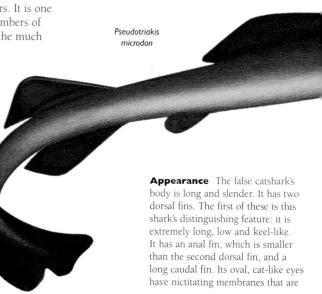

Appearance The false catshark's body is long and slender. It has two dorsal fins. The first of these is this shark's distinguishing feature: it is extremely long, low and keel-like. It has an anal fin, which is smaller than the second dorsal fin, and a long caudal fin. Its oval, cat-like eyes have nictitating membranes that are

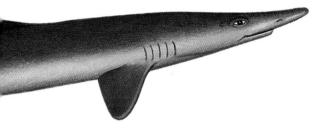

KEY FACTS

♀ 8¼ ft (2.5 m)

♂ 7½ ft (2.3 m)

Other names Dumb shark
Size at birth 3 ft (90 cm)
Maximum length 10 ft (3 m)
Diet Little known but probably large fish and invertebrates
Habitat A slope dweller at depths of 660–5,000 ft (200–1,500 m)
Distribution Patchy; in all tropical oceans and Hawaii and the North Atlantic

reduced in size. The spiracles behind the eyes are distinctively large. The false catshark has an enormous mouth and each of the jaws contains more than 200 rows of tiny teeth, well suited to catching the deepwater fishes and invertebrates that probably constitute its diet. The teeth at the back of the mouth are comb-like. This sluggish species is uniformly dark gray to dark brown with slightly darker fin margins.

Reproduction The false catshark is ovoviviparous. Females give birth to between two and four pups per litter. Recent research has shown that this species is also oophagous—embryos consume unfertilized eggs in the mother's uterus.

Comment Although it is common in some areas, divers hardly ever see this shark and very little is known about it.

BARBELED HOUNDSHARK

The barbeled houndshark is the only member of the unusual family Leptochariidae. While it closely resembles the true houndsharks and the finback catsharks, it differs from both in its longer labial furrows and in combining nearly circular eyes, minute spiracles and nostrils with barbels. It is also closely related to the requiem sharks. This small species is usually found in coastal areas, both inshore and above the adjacent shelf. It prefers muddy bottom areas, especially near river mouths, where it feeds on small fishes, crustaceans and cephalopods. Males have larger teeth than females. They may use these to grasp the females during copulation. The barbeled houndshark is fished commercially in west Africa for its meat and its skin.

Appearance The barbeled houndshark has a slender, elongated, tapering body. The first of two spineless dorsal fins is between the pectoral and pelvic fins. The second dorsal fin, which is significantly smaller than the first, is positioned above the anal fin, which itself is only slightly smaller than the second dorsal fin. There is a long caudal fin. This species lacks precaudal pits and its caudal fin has no strong ventral lobe. The head is small, the mouth long and the eyes are large and cat-like. The spiracles are tiny. The barbeled houndshark's nasal flaps are modified into short, slender barbels. The corners of the mouth have long labial furrows and both jaws are lined with small teeth—larger in the male than in the female—that have narrow cusps and cusplets. This shark is light gray to brown and is paler on the underside.

Reproduction This is a viviparous species in which females give birth to litters of about seven pups after a gestation period of four months.

Comment Barbeled houndsharks seem to be omnivores. Apart from their staple diet of fish, crustaceans and eggs, they scavenge after all kinds of seemingly inedible objects. Such unlikely "foods" as feathers and flowers have been found inside the stomachs of specimens that have been collected for study.

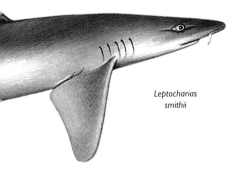

*Leptocharias
smithii*

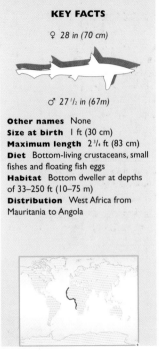

KEY FACTS

♀ 28 in (70 cm)

♂ 27 ¹/₂ in (67m)

Other names None
Size at birth 1 ft (30 cm)
Maximum length 2³/₄ ft (83 cm)
Diet Bottom-living crustaceans, small fishes and floating fish eggs
Habitat Bottom dweller at depths of 33–250 ft (10–75 m)
Distribution West Africa from Mauritania to Angola

TOPE SHARK

It was as recently as 1984 that what had been considered to be four separate species of sharks, distributed widely in cold and temperate waters in both hemispheres, were finally identified as belonging to a single species. This long-lived shark, which is thought to have a potential lifespan of about 60 years, has been shown to migrate long distances, presumably in order to allow pregnant females to give birth in cooler waters. The tope shark is fished for its meat, fin and liver oil. This, particularly in view of its longevity and low reproduction rate, puts the species at risk. Females reach maturity at eight to 10 years and breed only every second or third year.

Appearance Usually found on continental shelves and continental slopes in temperate waters, and generally absent in tropical waters, the tope shark generally feeds on fish, squid and octopus near the seabed or in the water column. This active shark, which spends most of its time swimming, has quite a slender body with two dorsal fins. The second of these dorsal fins is significantly smaller than the first, and is about the same size as the anal fin. The large subterminal lobe on the caudal fin can create the illusion that this shark has a double tail. The tope shark has a long snout and elongate eyes with nictitating eyelids. The coloring on the upper body is a bronzy gray. The underside is lighter in color.

Reproduction This ovoviviparous species gives birth in spring and early summer after a gestation period of one year. Litters vary from 15 to 50 pups. Larger females generally produce larger litters.

Comment This shark is thought to be harmless to humans, but divers have had little chance to test this theory. This very shy creature will usually flee long before a diver arrives in its vicinity. Newborn pups are sometimes caught by anglers.

Galeorhinus galeus

KEY FACTS

♀ 5 1/4 ft (1.6 m)

♂ 5 ft (1.5 m)

Other names Soupfin shark, school shark, vitamin shark, snapper shark
Size at birth 1 ft (30 cm)
Maximum length 6 1/2 ft (2 m)
Diet Mostly bony fishes, but also squid and octopus
Habitat Coastal, on bottom from shallow water to 1,800 ft (550 m)
Distribution Widespread in Pacific and Atlantic oceans, Mediterranean Sea, southern Australia and New Zealand

DUSKY SMOOTHHOUND

The dusky smoothhound is one of at least 37 species of houndsharks, members of the family Triakidae. It occurs mainly in temperate waters on continental and insular shelves from the shore down. Some dusky smoothhounds are also found on the continental slopes, as far as 1,900 feet (580 m) below the surface. Like most houndsharks, it displays a preference for mud, sand and rocky bottoms, commonly in enclosed bays. It never ventures into the open ocean. These sharks occasionally enter fresh water. They are abundant, and divers will often see them lying on the seabed in shallow coastal waters. Since they are completely harmless, they can be approached with perfect safety.

Appearance This shark is one of the larger houndsharks. While a few reach a maximum length of more than 6 feet (2 m), most do not grow to more than 4 feet (1.2 m). The dusky smoothhound is a slender shark with two large dorsal fins, set well apart. The first of these, situated in front of the pelvic fins, is significantly larger than the second. There is an anal fin, which is about half the size of the second dorsal fin,

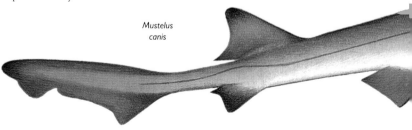

Mustelus canis

and a long caudal fin. The pectoral fins are broad and pointed. The snout is long and pointed and the nostrils have anterior flaps that are not formed as barbels. The eyes are small with nictitating membranes, and the spiracles are small. This shark is a uniform grayish brown above, and white on the underside.

Reproduction This species is viviparous, with a yolk-sac placenta. Females give birth to between four and 20 pups per litter.

Comment Dusky smoothhounds are able to change color to blend in with their environment. They survive well in captivity.

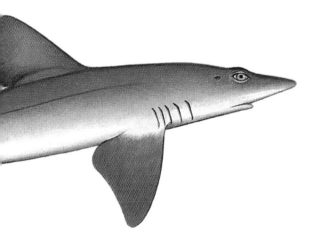

KEY FACTS

♂♀ 3 ½ ft (105 cm)

Other names None
Size at birth 13–15 in (33–38 cm)
Maximum length 5 ft (1.5 m)
Diet Primarily large crabs and lobsters; also shellfish, squid and small bony fishes
Habitat Continental shelves and slopes from near surface to 650 ft (200 m)
Distribution Western Atlantic from Massachusetts to Venezuela and from Brazil to Argentina; the Gulf of Mexico

LEOPARD SHARK

One of the houndsharks, a member of the family Triakidae, the leopard shark is a regular and conspicuous inhabitant of most bays along the coast of northern California. It survives well in captivity and its attractive markings make it a popular occupant of public aquariums. It is usually quite sluggish. Although they possess all the fins typical of a modern shark, leopard sharks do not need to swim in order to breathe. Each year they migrate from the inner bays to the outer coast of the temperate Pacific Northwest. They are harmless to humans, but because of their similar markings they are often mistaken for the dangerous tiger shark.

Appearance This sluggish shark has an attractive and elongated body, with a series of black spots and dark saddle-shaped markings over a bronze to golden brown background. Some individuals have stripes as well as spots on their bodies. The leopard shark has two dorsal fins of similar size (the first situated in front of the pelvic fins) and pointed pectoral fins. There is an anal fin that is smaller

Triakis semifasciata

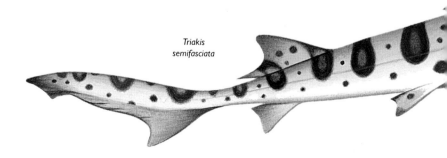

than the second dorsal fin and an asymmetrical caudal fin. There are no precaudal pits. This shark has oval eyes with nictitating membranes, a long snout, small spiracles and an impressive array of small, pointed teeth, which it uses to capture a wide variety of food. Its nostrils have anterior flaps which are not formed as barbels.

Reproduction This species is ovoviviparous, without a yolk-sac placenta. In spring, the female gives birth in coastal bays to between four and 29 pups per litter after a gestation period of one year.

Comment Because they are social and travel in schools, these sharks are often caught in large numbers.

KEY FACTS

♀ 5 ft (1.5 m)

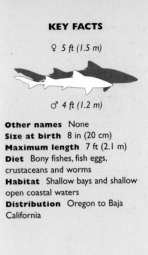

♂ 4 ft (1.2 m)

Other names None
Size at birth 8 in (20 cm)
Maximum length 7 ft (2.1 m)
Diet Bony fishes, fish eggs, crustaceans and worms
Habitat Shallow bays and shallow open coastal waters
Distribution Oregon to Baja California

ATLANTIC WEASEL SHARK

One of seven known members of the family Hemigaleidae, known collectively as weasel sharks, the Atlantic weasel shark is the only one that lives in the eastern Atlantic Ocean. The other members of this family are characteristic of the Indo-West Pacific, from South Africa and the Red Sea to Japan and Australia. The Atlantic weasel shark's small range and limited distribution mean that, though it is easily recognizable by its distinctive yellow stripes, it is rarely sighted and, so far at least, only poorly understood. Like the other weasel sharks, it is an inshore species, occurring in shelf waters at modest depths along the coast of west Africa.

Appearance The Atlantic weasel shark is a medium-sized shark that bears some resemblance to the requiem sharks. It has a slender body with two dorsal fins, which are set well apart. The first of these, situated in front of the pelvic fins, is significantly larger than the second. The pectoral fins are long and pointed and the anal fin is considerably smaller than the second dorsal fin. The asymmetrical caudal fin has a strong ventral lobe and

there are precaudal pits. This shark has a moderately long snout; large, oval (but almost round) eyes with nictitating membranes; a short, small mouth; small teeth; and minute spiracles. It is a uniform blue-gray to bronze color with distinctive yellow stripes on the top of its body, and white on the underside.

Reproduction Like all weasel sharks, this species is viviparous. Females give birth to between one and four pups per litter.

Comment The fact that it specializes in feeding upon soft-bodied cephalopods (squid and octopus) is reflected in its small mouth, small teeth and presumably suctorial feeding mechanism.

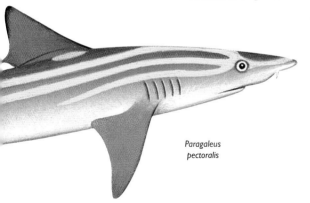

Paragaleus pectoralis

KEY FACTS

♂♀ 3¼ ft (1 m)

Other names None
Size at birth 16 in (40 cm)
Maximum length 4½ ft (1.4 m)
Diet Primarily squid and octopus; also small fishes
Habitat Shallow water to 330 ft (100 m)
Distribution Tropical western Africa

SILVERTIP SHARK

A member of the family Carcharhinidae, commonly known as requiem sharks, the silvertip gets its common name from the distinctive white tips and margins on its fins. Silvertip sharks prefer offshore islands, coral reefs and banks and adults typically inhabit waters below 82 feet (25 m). However, they also frequently enter lagoons, and it is here that they are most often encountered. These large, aggressive sharks often dominate other *Carcharhinus* species when feeding. They have been known to harass divers, but reports of attacks on people are rare.

Appearance The silvertip shark has a slender body. There are two dorsal fins (the first being much larger than the second); long, pointed pectoral fins; and an anal fin. The caudal fin is asymmetrical.

Carcharhinus albimarginatus

This shark has a moderately long, rounded snout and fairly small round eyes. There are no spiracles. Its teeth are similar to those of other *Carcharhinus* species. They are strongly serrated and narrowly pointed in the lower jaw, and sharp, serrated and oblique in the upper jaw. They are ideal for catching and cutting the fish that they feed upon, such as reef wrasses and, in open water, tuna and flying fishes. The upper side of the silvertip's body is bronze; the underside is paler. This shark's most distinguishing feature are the white tips on its pectoral, pelvic, caudal and first dorsal fins. These tips are absent on the anal and second dorsal fins.

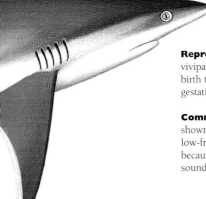

Reproduction This species is viviparous. Females usually give birth to five or six young after a gestation period of 12 months.

Comment Experiments have shown that silvertips are attracted to low-frequency sounds, probably because these frequencies mimic the sound made by an injured fish.

KEY FACTS

♂♀ *10 ft (3 m)*

Other names Silvertip whaler
Size at birth 2 1/8 ft (65 cm)
Maximum length 10 ft (3 m)
Diet Pelagic and bottom fishes
Habitat Along reef drop-offs from the surface to 2,625 ft (800 m)
Distribution Widespread in tropical Indo-Pacific; east coast of Africa from the Red Sea and South Africa eastward to the eastern Pacific; Mexico to Colombia

GRAY REEF SHARK

One of the requiem sharks, the gray reef shark is among the most common sharks on Indo-Pacific coral reefs and is often seen in the reef passes. An inquisitive, and potentially dangerous, shark, it is attracted to the low-frequency underwater sounds made by a speared fish—there are many stories of gray reef sharks taking fishes off the end of unsuspecting spearfishers' spears. Attacks against potential enemies are preceded by a complex warning display that involves head wagging, depressed pectoral fins and an arched back.

Appearance This shark is familiar to any diver on Indo-Pacific reefs and has a shape typical of most requiem species. It has a distinctive black banding on the posterior margin of its caudal fin. Some specimens also have a narrow white edging on the first dorsal fin. The second dorsal fin is much smaller than the first and there is an anal fin. The caudal fin is quite large and asymmetrical. The gray reef shark has a long snout, round eyes and no spiracles. Its teeth are triangular and finely serrated. The top part of the body is bronze to gray, and the underside is white.

Reproduction The species is viviparous. Females give birth to litters of one to six pups after a gestation period of 12 months.

Comment Male gray reef sharks display a remarkable ability to recognize females of the species by smell. Males have been observed moving along apparent odor trails produced by females.

Carcharhinus amblyrhynchos

KEY FACTS

♂♀ 6 ft (1.8 m)

Other names Black-V, whaler, longnosed blacktail shark
Size at birth 20 in (50 cm)
Maximum length 8 ½ ft (2.6 m)
Diet Primarily reef fishes
Habitat Reef drop-offs and passes; occasionally on the reef top
Distribution Tropical Indo-Pacific, from Hawaii westward

GALAPAGOS SHARK

This large, grayish requiem shark was named in 1905 after specimens found in the waters of the Galapagos Islands. It has since been found around most tropical oceanic islands, ranging from inshore to well offshore. It prefers clear water, and can be seen beyond the deep reef edge, either near the surface or swimming in groups near the bottom. It feeds primarily on bottom-dwelling fishes, squid and octopus. This potentially aggressive shark does not normally attack humans, but a number of fatal attacks against swimmers have been recorded.

Appearance The Galapagos shark is a typical requiem shark with a stocky body and a low, but prominent, ridge between its dorsal fins. This ridge is its most distinctive feature, but divers would be wise not to get close enough to make it out. However, this shark lacks the conspicuous white or black marking on the fins that are characteristic of other requiem sharks. The Galapagos shark has large pectoral fins with narrow, rounded tips. It has a high

first dorsal fin and a second dorsal fin that is similar in size to the anal fin. Its snout is long and rounded, its eyes are round and there are no spiracles. The body is charcoal gray to brown with a pale, almost white underside. Most of the fins have dusky tips that fade with age.

Reproduction This species is viviparous. Females give birth in shallow water to between six and 16 pups per litter.

Comment Like the gray reef shark, the Galapagos shark performs a seemingly awkward threat display before attacking a potential competitor or predator.

Carcharhinus galapagensis

KEY FACTS

♀ 9 ft (2.7 m)

♂ 7½ ft (2.3 m)

Other names None
Size at birth 23–32 in (57–80 cm)
Maximum length 12 ft (3.6 m)
Diet Reef fishes
Habitat Just beyond outer reef edge
Distribution Cosmopolitan in tropics, generally near oceanic islands

BULL SHARK

This large, sluggish gray shark is widespread along continental coasts. It also enters rivers and lakes. The bull shark can tolerate highly salty sea water and fresh water and has been recorded far up the Mississippi and Amazon rivers. It will eat almost anything it can capture. Because it has been confused with other requiem sharks, it may well have been responsible for more attacks than it has been credited with. It is, perhaps, the most lethal of all sharks.

Appearance The bull shark has a unique appearance. It gets its common name from its broad, rounded snout, which is reminiscent of the snout of a bull. It has a heavy body, broad pectoral fins with pointed tips and two dorsal fins, the first of which is significantly larger than the second. It lacks the interdorsal ridge and distinctive fin markings that are

Carcharhinus leucas

characteristic of requiem sharks. It has large jaws; triangular, sharp, serrated teeth; round eyes; and no spiracles. Its coloring is grey on the top of the body and white on the underside. Juveniles have dark tips on their fins.

Reproduction The bull shark is viviparous, mating in late spring and summer, and giving birth in shallow waters to between one and 13 pups per litter after a gestation period of 10 to 11 months.

Comment Because they live close inshore and in rivers and lakes, they are vulnerable to fisheries.

KEY FACTS

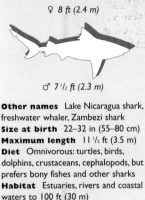

♀ 8 ft (2.4 m)

♂ 7 ½ ft (2.3 m)

Other names Lake Nicaragua shark, freshwater whaler, Zambezi shark
Size at birth 22–32 in (55–80 cm)
Maximum length 11 ½ ft (3.5 m)
Diet Omnivorous: turtles, birds, dolphins, crustaceans, cephalopods, but prefers bony fishes and other sharks
Habitat Estuaries, rivers and coastal waters to 100 ft (30 m)
Distribution All tropical and subtropical seas

OCEANIC WHITETIP SHARK

This large requiem shark is usually found far offshore. In the open ocean it can often be seen from boats or encountered by divers. It is most abundant in the tropics, but can also be found from southern California to southern Australia, following the warm water masses. It will eat almost anything it can find in the open sea, including whale carcasses and garbage dumped from ships.

Carcharhinus longimanus

Appearance The oceanic whitetip shark has a stocky body with two dorsal fins, long pectoral fins and a low interdorsal ridge. The enlarged, rounded first dorsal fin and the paddle-shaped pectoral fins are unmistakable features of this species. These fins—and often the tip of the lower lobe of the caudal fin—have conspicuous, mottled, white tips. The fins of juveniles may also have black markings. The oceanic whitetip shark has a short, broad, rounded snout; triangular, sharp, serrated teeth; round eyes; and no spiracles. The upper body is brownish gray, fading to white on the underside.

Reproduction This species is viviparous. Females give birth to between six and 15 pups per litter. The gestation period is 12 months.

Comment These aggressive sharks will dominate other shark species that are competing for food. They are also very dangerous to humans and, although generally sluggish, are capable of short bursts of speed.

KEY FACTS

♀ 7 ½ ft (2.3 m)

♂ 7 ft (2.1 m)

Other names
Whitetip whaler, whitetip shark
Size at Birth 2 ½ ft (75 cm)
Maximum length 13 ft (4 m)
Diet Wide-ranging, including fishes, squid, birds, turtles and carrion
Habitat Offshore, from the surface to 500 ft (150 m)
Distribution All tropical and subtropical seas

BLACKTIP REEF SHARK

Blacktip reef sharks are among the most common sharks in the shallow lagoons and coral reefs of the tropical Pacific and Indian oceans. Divers and snorkelers often see these sharks patrolling in shallow waters from about 1 foot (30 cm) deep. Divers will find them in reef passes; waders and snorkelers will see them in lagoons, their dorsal and caudal fins above the surface. Because they are a small, hardy species, a number of these sharks have been captured in the central Pacific, off Christmas Island, and sent to public aquariums worldwide.

Appearance This smallish shark has a thick body, with two dorsal fins (the second is significantly shorter than the first), but no interdorsal ridge. There is an anal fin and an asymmetrical caudal fin. Blacktip reef sharks are easily recognized by the very distinct black marks at the tips

Carcharhinus melanopterus

of their fins, particularly those on the first dorsal and caudal fins. They also have a conspicuous white slash along their flanks. The eyes are large, there are no spiracles and the snout is short and rounded. The teeth are narrow, sharp and strongly serrated. This shark is yellowish brown to gray, with a white underside.

Reproduction This species is viviparous. Females give birth in shallow waters to between two and four pups per litter after a gestation period of eight to nine months.

Comment While not considered dangerous to divers, the blacktip reef shark has been known to bite waders on the legs and ankles, probably attracted by the splashing.

KEY FACTS

♂ 4 1/2 ft (1.4 m)

♀ 3 2/3 ft (1.1 m)

Other names
Blacktip shark, guliman
Size at birth 20 in (50 cm)
Maximum length 6 ft (1.8 m)
Diet Primarily reef fishes, but also crustaceans and cephalopods
Habitat Shallow reef flats to outer reef edge
Distribution Tropical central Pacific to eastern Africa; entered the Mediterranean through Suez Canal

TIGER SHARK

This large, dangerous shark is to tropical waters what the great white shark, *Carcharodon carcharias,* is to temperate waters. One of the few true shark scavengers, it has eaten cattle, pigs, donkeys, sheep and humans that have fallen overboard. Adult tiger sharks spend their days beyond the reef edge, except at certain times of the year, when they also come inshore during the day. They are active at night, and enter shallow reefs and lagoons to feed. In some areas they migrate between island groups to take advantage of colonies of young birds learning to fly over water. Tiger sharks live for about 12 years.

Appearance The tiger shark has a large, barrel-shaped body that tapers to a slender section in front of its well-developed, long, pointed caudal fin. It has a large, flattened head; a broad, blunt snout; and a wide mouth. Small spiracles are located just behind the eyes. Each of its jaws contains 18 to 20 rows of heavily serrated, cockscomb-shaped teeth, which allow it to cut through the bodies of large sea turtles, as well as seals, and cetaceans. The upper body is bluish gray to brown, and the underside is yellow to light gray or white. The tiger shark is so named because the body is covered with black or dark gray vertical stripes that fade with maturity.

Reproduction This is the only requiem shark that is ovoviviparous. Female tiger sharks give birth to 10 to 82 pups per litter after a gestation period of 12 to 13 months.

Comment This usually slow swimmer is capable of short bursts of speed when feeding. The species is rarely sighted.

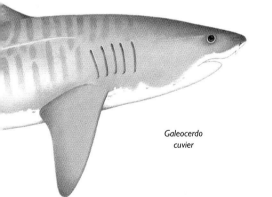

Galeocerdo cuvier

KEY FACTS

♀ 12 ft (3.7 m)

♂ 10 ft (3 m)

Other names None
Size at birth 20–30 in (50–75 cm)
Maximum length 24 ft (7.3 m)
Diet Extremely wide-ranging, including turtles, fishes, seals, birds, carrion and virtually anything that falls overboard
Habitat Inshore along coral and rocky reefs at night and beyond the reef edge to 500 ft (150 m) in daytime
Distribution Worldwide in tropics

LEMON SHARK

This shark is abundant in tropical reef systems, especially those with sea grass and associated mangrove habitats. It is highly tolerant of shallow waters with low oxygen levels, such as warm-water mangrove swamps or bays, places where it is commonly observed. Lemon sharks are active throughout the day and night. Some populations seem to undertake long migrations in search of food, because they are found in summer along continental shelves and sandy beaches in areas of high latitudes.

Appearance This sluggish shark has a stocky body with two large dorsal fins, the second of which is almost as large as the first. These dorsal fins are an identifying feature of the species. There is a large anal fin, immediately below the second dorsal fin, and broad pectoral fins that curve back on the trailing edge. Its head is broad and flattened, its snout is short and it has smooth, dagger-like teeth. Occasionally there are vestigial spiracles. Its coloring is pale yellow, light brown or mustard, which fades to a lemon yellow or white on the underside. There are no obvious markings.

Reproduction The species is viviparous, mating in spring and summer. The gestation period is 14 months (shorter in warmer areas). Females give birth in shallow waters to litters of four to 17 pups.

Comment This species survives well in captivity and has been well researched. It is harmless to humans unless provoked.

KEY FACTS

♀ 8 1/2 ft (2.6 m)

♂ 8 1/4 ft (2.5 m)

Other names None
Size at birth 2 ft (60 cm)
Maximum length 11 ft (3.4 m)
Diet Bony fishes, rays, crustaceans and mollusks
Habitat Shallow sea grass beds and mangrove flats
Distribution Western Atlantic from New Jersey to Brazil; possibly eastern Atlantic; eastern Pacific from Baja California to Ecuador

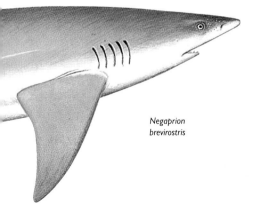

Negaprion brevirostris

BLUE SHARK

One of the most attractive of sharks, the blue shark is found in the open ocean throughout the tropics and into cooler seas. In the tropics it often enters deeper, cooler water, while in temperate coastal waters it comes close to the edge of kelp beds, where divers may see it. It migrates regularly in the Atlantic, following the Gulf Stream to Europe, moving south along the African coast, then returning to the Caribbean. Once the most plentiful shark in the sea, it is now endangered through overfishing. It will attack humans without being provoked.

Appearance A very easily recognizable species because of its striking coloration, the blue shark has a long, slender body with two dorsal fins. However, it lacks the interdorsal ridge that characterizes many requiem sharks. Its pectoral fins are long, pointed and narrow.

It has a narrow head; a long, narrow snout; and large eyes with a white rim. In some individuals there are vestigial spiracles. Its teeth are serrated and triangular. The upper body is a bright indigo blue; the flanks are paler, but still bright blue; and the underside, in contrast, is distinctly white.

Reproduction The species is viviparous. After a gestation period of nine to 12 months, females give birth in the open ocean. An average litter size is about 40, but litters as large as 135 have been observed.

Comment During courtship, males bite the females, which have much thicker skin, on the shoulders. Females store the sperm for nearly a year, after which fertilization occurs.

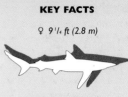

KEY FACTS

♀ 9 ¼ ft (2.8 m)

♂ 8 ¼ ft (2.5 m)

Other names Blue whaler, great blue shark, blue dog
Size at birth 16 in (40 cm)
Maximum length 12 ½ ft (3.9 m)
Diet Pelagic fishes, squid and krill
Habitat Oceanic, from the surface to 1,150 ft (350 m); close to shore in some locations
Distribution All tropical and temperate seas

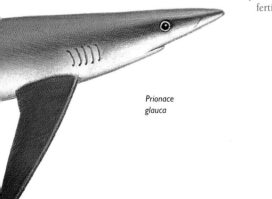

*Prionace
glauca*

WHITETIP REEF SHARK

These sluggish, fairly slender requiem sharks live close to shore, usually at depths of between 26 and 130 feet (8–40 m). During the day, divers predictably find them resting in caves, particularly in Hawaii and the Galapagos Islands, or under rock or coral ledges. They are active at night and during slack tides. They can become accustomed to the sounds of boats and to spearfishers, and are aroused by the presence of divers, whom they approach out of curiosity. Although they are not aggressive to humans, these sharks need to be approached with caution. Some foolhardy divers have been badly bitten when feeding them squid and fishes.

Appearance The whitetip reef shark has a slender body with two dorsal fins. The second of these is almost equal in size to the anal fin. The pectoral and dorsal fins have pointed tips. This shark gets its common name from the conspicuous white tips on its dorsal and caudal fins. The head is broad, the snout is short and rounded and occasionally there are vestigial spiracles. The teeth are medium-sized with smooth edges, which are flanked by small cusps. It uses these teeth to grip and pull fish prey out of hiding places in reef crevices. Coloring is gray to brown above, fading to a pale underside. Dark blotches are sometimes splattered on the body.

Reproduction This species is viviparous. Females give birth to from one to five pups per litter after a gestation period of 13 months.

Comment The flesh and liver of whitetip reef sharks are consumed by humans. It is unique among sharks in having caused ciguatera poisoning— a type of food poisoning with severe gastrointestinal symptoms.

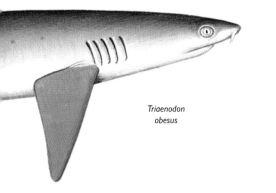

Triaenodon obesus

KEY FACTS

♂ 4 ½ ft (1.4 m)

♀ 4 ¼ ft (1.3 m)

Other names Blunthead shark
Size at birth 21–24 in (52–60 cm)
Maximum length 7 ft (2.1 m)
Diet Bottom fishes, crustaceans and cephalopods
Habitat A shallow-water reef dweller, to depths of 1,000 ft (300 m)
Distribution Tropical eastern Pacific to eastern Africa; widespread in Oceania

221

SCALLOPED HAMMERHEAD

This shark belongs to a family, Sphyrnidae, of eight sharks with a unique specialization—the front of the skull expands laterally like a hammer to form a head structure called a cephalofoil. This serves many biological functions. Its wide, flattened shape adds lift during swimming and the position of the eyes at the tips of the head help these large, active sharks to capture large or elusive prey. They occur in coastal areas above continental and island shelves and in adjacent offshore waters. They often enter shallow bays and estuaries. Here divers see them interacting in a vigorous manner—chasing, thrusting, shaking their heads and biting each other.

Appearance Scalloped hammerheads can be distinguished by the broad leading edge on the head, which is arched toward the back. There is a prominent indentation in the center, with two smaller lobes on either side, giving the head a scalloped look. The eyes

Sphyrna lewini

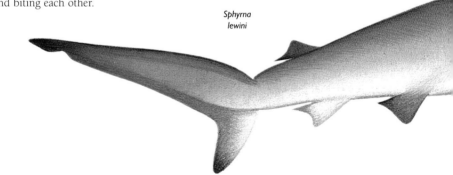

and nostrils are located on the tips of this "hammer" head. There are two dorsal fins, small pectoral fins and an anal fin. Scalloped hammerheads vary in color from deep olive green, through brown and bronze, to gray. Their pectoral fins often have charcoal gray to black tips.

Reproduction The scalloped hammerhead is viviparous, with a yolk-sac placenta. Females give birth in shallow waters to litters of from 15 to 30 pups, after a gestation period of nine to 10 months.

Comment This is probably the most abundant of the hammerhead sharks. It is often seen in large schools and presents little risk to humans.

KEY FACTS

♀ 8 ½ ft (2.6 m)

♂ 7 ft (2.1 m)

Other names Kidney-headed shark, bronze hammerhead
Size at birth 17–22 in (43–55 cm)
Maximum length 12 ft (3.7 m), possibly larger
Diet Bony fishes and squid
Habitat Coastal, from the surface to 900 ft (270 m)
Distribution Worldwide in tropical and warm-temperate seas

GREAT HAMMERHEAD

This species is distributed in nearly all warm temperate and tropical waters. It occurs in coastal areas above continental island shelves and in adjacent offshore waters. Divers are likely to see it in shallow waters, especially near coral reef drop-offs and adjacent sand habitats. It makes long migrations to cooler waters during the summer. The great hammerhead is an impressive predator. Its diet consists of many mobile fishes associated with the water column and benthic creatures such as grouper, sea cats and flatfishes. But it is best known as a hunter of stingrays, skates and other sharks.

Appearance The great hammerhead has a moderately slender body with two dorsal fins. The first of these is extremely high and pointed with a curved rear margin. The base of the anal fin is much longer than that of the second dorsal fin. The species has a distinctive hammer-shaped head, which is straight at the front margin except for one indentation in the middle, with nostrils and eyes on the tips of the hammer. Coloring is bronze to grayish brown or dark olive, and the underside is lighter.

Reproduction The great hammerhead is viviparous. Females give birth in late spring to summer after an 11-month gestation period. Litter sizes vary from six to 33. The size of the litter is directly related to the size of the female.

Comment The great hammerhead's keen olfactory sense helps it to track its prey. Unlike most other hammerhead sharks, this species does pose a danger to humans and has attacked on occasion.

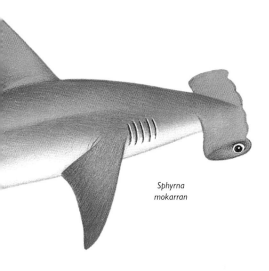

*Sphyrna
mokarran*

♂ 12 ft (3.7 m)

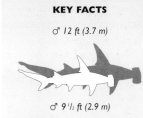

♂ 9 ¹/₂ ft (2.9 m)

Other names Scoop hammerhead
Size at Birth 2 ¹/₃ ft (65 cm)
Maximum length 20 ft (6.1 m)
Diet Other sharks and rays
Habitat Coastal and above continental shelves, from surface to 260 ft (80 m)
Distribution All tropical seas; not found in Hawaii

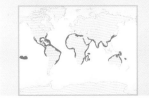

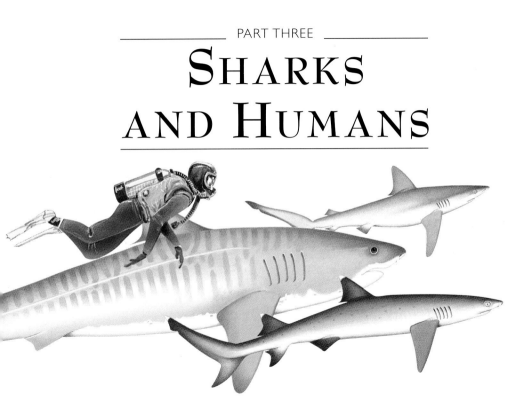

PART THREE

SHARKS
AND HUMANS

SHARK ATTACK

There have been reports of sharks attacking people since the time of the ancient Greeks. Such attacks have probably been occurring for as long as people have been entering the water. Shark attacks are traditionally broken down into two categories—provoked and unprovoked. Provoked attacks are usually cases of sharks defending themselves against deliberate or inadvertent human interference. While unfortunate, such attacks are not particularly surprising. Unprovoked attacks, on the other hand, occur unpredictably and still pose something of a mystery.

WHY SHARKS ATTACK

Most shark attacks on humans are prompted by two basic situations. First, there are attacks related to threat and aggression. Second, there are attacks related to feeding, in which the shark approaches the victim as a potential meal. Attacks in the first group are either provoked or unprovoked. Those in the second are usually associated with large species.

An attack database In 1958, at the instigation of the United States Navy, a panel of scientists began to compile a worldwide historical database of shark attacks. By 1996 this database was known as the International Shark Attack File and contained details of more than 1,800 confirmed attacks. Between 75 and 100 new cases are added to the file each year, of which fewer than 20 are fatal. Unfortunately, due to the patchy information supplied from some countries, the information contained and recorded is not a complete record.

Provoked attacks Provoked attacks that are related to threat and aggression are usually the result of divers showing very poor judgment in relating to the sharks they encounter. Pulling the tail of a whitetip reef shark as it rests in an

HUMANS AT RISK
Most shark attacks occur close to shore, which is not surprising given that most water users swim among the breakers. The great white shark (far left) has been implicated in many attacks on humans. The silvertip reef shark (far right) is potentially dangerous to divers.

underwater cave, for example, or attempting to hand-feed it, or members of other dangerous species, are examples of blatantly provocative behavior. In the same way, any fisher who is bitten by a landed shark is considered to have provoked the "attack."

Unprovoked attacks
Unprovoked attacks occur when victims blunder unintentionally into the behavioral sphere of a shark and seem to threaten it with harm. For example, a surfer or windsurfer may speed into the an area where a reef shark is swimming. If the surfer falls from the board near the shark, the shark will lash out to meet the perceived "threat."

Feeding Shark attacks are often attributed to feeding behavior, and sharks may be provoked by food stimuli in the water, such as blood from speared fishes. One explanation that has been proposed for unprovoked attacks is that sharks mistake people gathering on the surface for their usual prey. However, it is open to debate whether or not a shark actually mistakes a person for particular kind of prey. It may be enough that the person is at the surface of the water where many species find much of their food., whether it be fishes, marine mammals or carrion. Defense, threat and feeding account for many attacks, but they do not explain them all. We can look for common themes, but we will never know all the circumstances that lead a shark to attack a human.

WHY SHARKS ATTACK continued

Sharks that attack humans

Sharks tend to attack as individuals rather than in groups, and it is not always possible to determine exactly what species was responsible for a given attack. However, while more than 30 species of sharks have been implicated in attacks on humans, the vast majority of fatal attacks appear to be carried out by only three of these—the great white, tiger and bull sharks. What makes these sharks dangerous to humans are their large size, their varied prey, their ability to capture large prey and their tendency

to inhabit those near shore areas where people most often work and play.

Coastline attacks White sharks are common along rocky shorelines where seals and sea lions crawl up onto the shore. These are areas also favored by surfers and divers. Tiger sharks are often found around shallow reefs, harbors and stream mouths, and it is around such areas that people live in the greatest concentrations. Bull sharks, which are normally considered a coastal species, are also found in locations where most people would not expect to find a shark, such as freshwater rivers and estuaries. It should be noted, however, that none of these species includes humans as an important part of their diet and that aggressive encounters with any of them are not common.

A TASTE FOR TURTLES
Tropical tiger sharks (above) pose a danger to humans. They have a diverse diet but are known to feed on large sea turtles, including the hawksbill turtle (far left). It is probably good judgment to avoid swimming in areas where these and other sea turtles abound.

Open-ocean attacks The majority of open-ocean attacks are thought to be the work of oceanic whitetip sharks, although blue sharks are also thought to pose a risk to

DANGER
A diver (above right) takes a risk in hand-feeding a gray reef shark. Gray reef sharks have a complex threat ritual, which experienced divers can easily identify and, if necessary, take evasive action. Big-game fishers (above) proudly display the jaws of a conquered great white.

people stranded at sea. Non-fatal attacks near the shore have been attributed to smaller species, such as Caribbean and gray reef sharks. In many cases a surfer or swimmer has been bitten on the arm or foot—attacks termed "hit and runs" because the shark takes a bite, then flees. Such attacks may merely be cases of an inquisitive shark investigating a person in the water and then swimming off when it realizes that the victim was not the prey it was looking for.

Chances of attack Of the almost 500 species of shark, only 30 or so have been responsible for attacks on humans. So even if you swim in waters inhabited by sharks every day, the chances of being attacked are extremely low. Many more people are killed annually by dogs, crocodiles, elephants and even pigs than by sharks. Even in Australian waters, where the highest number of shark attacks per capita have been recorded, you are much more likely to drown than be attacked by a shark. Of all recorded cases of shark attack, only about 30 percent have been fatal. Furthermore, as the cause of death in most attacks is shock and loss of blood, fatalities have decreased greatly in the last 50 years due to better and more rapid application of first aid, and the improved treatment of post-traumatic infection.

Why the fear? If attacks are so rare, why is there such a fear of sharks? Perhaps it is because we don't understand them and cannot control them. On land we have established our dominance, but in the water we are literally out of our depth and even our intellect cannot help us overcome what evolution has perfected over 450 million years. Whatever the reason, it is important to remind ourselves that sharks are only doing what they have always done in an environment where we are very much the intruders.

MYTHS AND TRUTHS

The primal fear of being devoured by a predator is deeply rooted in our psyche. In marine environments, sharks are the creatures that people traditionally have feared more than any others. Our attitudes toward sharks have always been colored by the fact that some species do in fact kill humans.

Changing attitudes Although some sharks are still justifiably objects of fear, as people have learned more about the complexity of sharks and their behavior patterns, the collective attitude has become far more enlightened. Certainly, mixed into every personal point of view is a healthy respect and a fundamental fear, but our feelings toward sharks today are very different from those of past generations. Only a half-century ago, there were few opportunities for the general public (or, for that matter, even scientists) to see even mediocre photographs of sharks.

FRUSTRATED PREDATOR
To observe great whites and similar potentially dangerous species at close quarters, groups of divers usually take refuge in the safety of a steel cage which can be winched to the surface if one of these powerful animals succeeds in damaging the bars.

Today, books, magazines, television and the Internet afford a treasure-house of sharp color images of sharks and other marine animals. A generation ago, to swim with sharks was to engage in the pursuits of a lunatic, or at least of a bold adventurer whose accounts were the stuff of sensational tales. Thanks to such adventurous spirits, prevailing attitudes are much better informed. People generally now understand that most shark species have little interest in humans as potential prey and that the chance of being attacked by a shark, even among avid surf enthusiasts, is small. This realization, however, should not be a cause for complacency.

Knowing the odds Entering any environment, especially one that is not natural to humans, is a gamble, and swimmers and other water users should always consider the odds. Thanks to the International Shark Attack File, there is fairly good, and

HARMLESS UNLESS PROVOKED

Wobbegongs, of which there are six species, are common on rocky and coral reefs, especially around the Australian and Papua New Guinea coasts. They are seemingly inoffensive sharks but have been implicated in attacks when provoked or disturbed by divers.

readily available, historical information on the frequency of shark attacks in particular locations. It must also be understood, though, that as human populations increase and as more people enter the sea for their livelihood and recreation, greater numbers are exposed to the danger of attack.

How many sharks? How many sharks of the kind implicated in shark attack are there in the sea? We don't know but, given increased fishing catches, there are probably fewer than there were a decade or more ago. A statistical analysis of shark attacks in selected coastal areas worldwide where there was significant

human activity in the sea, indicated that between 1990 and 1996 there were on average 50 shark attacks per year, six of which were fatal. That, surely, is a figure that should put our fears in perspective.

235

CREATING A MYTH: *JAWS*

The shark has long featured in Pacific myths. It had little symbolic significance, however, in other cultures, appearing only in natural histories or seafarers' journals. It was not until fairly recently that the shark captured the Western imagination.

A legend begins In 1974 the reputation of the shark took a quantum leap forward—or backward if you will. In that year Peter Benchley wrote *Jaws*, a novel that has as its main character, not a human, but a fish—and not just any fish, but a great white shark. Benchley was not the first to contribute to the great

LARGER THAN LIFE
The shark that was built to represent the marauding great white in the film *Jaws* and its sequels was 3 feet (90 cm) longer than the largest ever recorded real great white. Its teeth were deliberately oversized to add to the impact of the shark's appearance on screen.

white's elevation to totemic status. As early as 1916, reports of a series of shark attacks in New Jersey vied for newspaper space with the World War I Battle of the Somme in France. Four people died in the New Jersey surf within a period of three weeks and another lost a leg. Although these attacks were attributed to the great white, the identity of the attacking shark (or more likely, sharks) was never proved. Later interpretations favor the bull shark as the culprit, but the great white got the credit at the time.

The *Jaws* myth The novel *Jaws* was a smashing success, selling hundreds of thousands of copies around the world and the movie made from the book in 1975 was a blockbuster—for a while it was the highest grossing film in Hollywood history. On the cover of its June 23

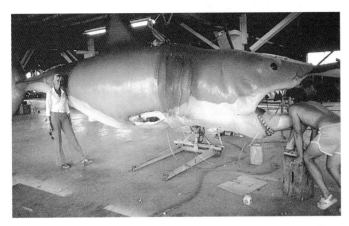

CREATING A LEGEND
Australian underwater film-maker Valerie Taylor stands beside one of the three mechanical sharks, collectively named Bruce, created for the *Jaws* films.

were reviewed by H. David Baldridge in a popular book called *Shark Attack,* published in 1975, the jacket copy stated "True tales of shark attacks on man—facts more terrifying than the fiction of *Jaws*."

The archetypal shark For millions of people the great white is truly the shark of myth. It is big, powerful, dangerous and frightening to behold. It has all the features that characterize the voracious shark: razor-sharp serrated teeth; menacing black eyes; a swift turn of speed; and, of course, that triangular dorsal fin, always "knifing" through the water. It is one of the few animals on Earth or in water that we fear can— or will—devour us. And that is the stuff of which legends are made.

1975 issue, *Time* magazine featured a shark bursting out of the water accompanied by the headline "Supershark." The edition's story on the making of the film capitalized on the popular image of the great white as "one of nature's most efficient killing machines." The movie's box-office success sparked a worldwide wave of shark attack hysteria.

The legend continues *Jaws II* followed hard on the heels of the original film, but did not repeat either its box-office or its critical success. *Jaws III* later limped into cinemas, an ineffectual shadow of either of its predecessors. However, the myth of the great white persisted in the popular imagination. When the findings of the Shark Attack File

237

WHERE SHARKS ATTACK

Not surprisingly, most shark attacks occur where people and sharks are most likely to come into contact. Shark attacks have been recorded between 58°N and 46°S latitude, equivalent of Scotland and New Zealand. However, the peaks in attacks occur between 32°N and 34°S—the area most densely populated by both humans and sharks.

Warm coastlines Per capita, the greatest recorded number of shark attacks have occurred in Australia, the United States and South Africa. These countries all have extensive coastlines within the peak latitudes and have seasonally warm temperatures. Because the majority of shark attacks have occurred in these areas, it was once assumed that dangerous sharks prefer warm water. However, dangerous sharks are common in colder waters too; it is just that people are less inclined to join them.

CLOSE INSHORE

Over 60 percent of shark attacks occur in water less than 5 feet (1.5 m) deep. This is not surprising given that most people who enter the water do so as swimmers, surfers and snorkelers, and seldom venture far offshore. Shark attack statistics tell us almost as much about the habits of people as those of sharks.

On and under the surface Most shark attacks occur close to shore, with approximately 31 percent of victims being within 50 feet (15 m) of the water's edge. However, were people to swim, or find themselves stranded, in the open ocean, they would certainly be vulnerable to attack. Statistics show that more than 90 percent of reported shark attacks occur on the surface. Although relatively few people venture underwater, figures suggest that these divers run a disproportionate risk of being attacked.

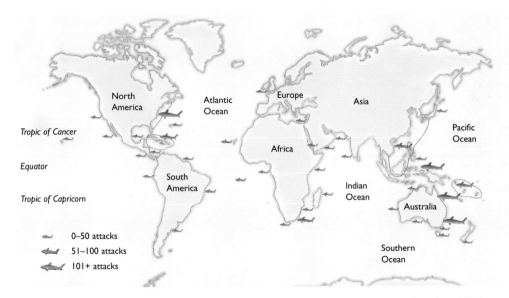

North America

Atlantic Ocean

Europe

Asia

Pacific Ocean

Tropic of Cancer

Africa

Equator

South America

Indian Ocean

Tropic of Capricorn

Australia

0–50 attacks

51–100 attacks

101+ attacks

Southern Ocean

SHARK ATTACK DISTRIBUTION
This map shows the relative worldwide distribution of authenticated cases of shark attack on humans that are recorded in the International Shark Attack File, a compilation of all known shark attacks, administered by the American Elasmobranch Society and the Florida Museum of Natural History. The file contains a record of more than 3,000 investigations, from the mid-1500s to the present. However, it is possible that language barriers and other factors have resulted in the true level of attack being understated in some areas.

ATTACK IN NORTH AMERICA

The International Shark Attack File classifies shark attack incidents as either "provoked" or "unprovoked" and additionally segregates attacks on boats from those directly involving humans. In this chapter we will address only unprovoked attacks—those cases where attacks occur in the shark's natural habitat without human provocation.

"Hit-and-run" attack These usually occur in the surf or wash zone. The victim is grabbed and quickly released by a shark. Injuries typically occur on extremities of the body and the shark does not return to make a repeat attack. Hit-and-run attacks are largely cases of mistaken identity, when sharks interpret provocative human actions (such

HAMMERHEADS
Species of hammerhead sharks have been identified in attacks in Atlantic waters. To some extent, however, the incidence of attack by hammerheads has been overstated, because their distinctive head shapes make them instantly recognizable.

as splashing of hand and feet at the surface) as schooling bait fishes breaking the water surface. These attacks are most common along the US Atlantic coast.

"Sneak" and "bump-and-bite" attacks Sharks are larger in these types of attacks, which generally occur in deeper water and frequently

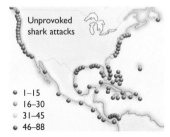

Unprovoked shark attacks
- 1–15
- 16–30
- 31–45
- 46–88

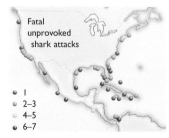

Fatal unprovoked shark attacks
- 1
- 2–3
- 4–5
- 6–7

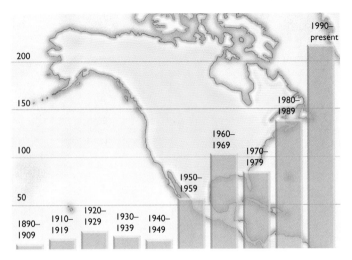

The graphs show the number of unprovoked attacks in North and Central American waters in 10-year spans, from 1890 to the present. The higher number of recent attacks reflects the greater number of people using the oceans for recreational activities.

Fatalities There have been 84 deaths in the region attributable to unprovoked shark attack (12 percent of 703 attacks). The highest mortality rate has occurred in Mexico and Central America, where emergency medical care lags behind that of other areas. By contrast, fatalities are much less common on the Atlantic and Pacific coasts of the United States. In parts of the region fatality rates have declined dramatically over the years with improvements in medical treatment. As evidence of this, the pre-1950 fatality rate of 44 percent for attacks in the insular Atlantic and US East Coast has been reduced to 2 percent since 1950.

involve repetitive bites. In sneak attacks, the shark is not observed before the unexpected first bite. In a bump-and-bite attack, the shark circles and often bumps the victim before biting. These types of attacks almost certainly represent feeding or aggressive behaviors. It seems unlikely that sharks seek out humans as prey items; humans simply approximate, size and shape, normal food items. All regional deaths recorded to date have been the result of bump-and-bite and sneak attacks.

Where sharks attack Shark attacks have been reported from all North and Central American countries except Belize, Guatemala, Honduras and Nicaragua. It is likely that attacks have occurred in these countries but no authenticated incidents have been recorded, although there have been unverified Lake Nicaragua attacks. As might be expected, attacks are more common in warmer waters, where sharks and humans are more abundant.

Attacks by Caribbean reef sharks

• 1
• 2

The Atlantic coast The sole Canadian Atlantic coast attack was reported from Newfoundland. Twelve attacks have occurred in the northeastern United States, from Massachusetts to New York, and 26 in the Middle Atlantic Bight, from New Jersey to Virginia. There have been 49 attacks in the South Atlantic Bight, from North Carolina to Georgia. Of those, 32 occurred in South Carolina, more than any state other than Florida and California.

Attacks by spinner sharks

• 3

Attacks by hammerhead sharks

• 1
• 2
• 8

Florida Florida leads the region in shark attacks and has averaged 17 attacks per year since 1990. This high incidence can be attributed in part to its very long coastline and inshore waters that are high in biological productivity and habitat diversity. The shark fauna is rich and, until recently, populations have been robust. The state has a rapidly growing resident population, augmented by year-round influxes of tourists. Two-thirds of Florida's attacks have occurred in the last two decades, mirroring the trends in population and tourism growth.

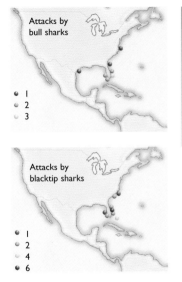

Attacks by
bull sharks

● 1
● 2
● 3

Attacks by
blacktip sharks

● 1
● 2
● 4
● 6

The southeast Atlantic The
remaining countries in the
southeastern part of the region have
had 96 attacks, with the Bahamas
(33) and Mexico (19) recording the

most. More than 80 percent of the
attacks in the Bahamas have occurred
in the 1980s and 1990s, largely
because of increased spearfishing
and ecotourism sharkfeeding
dives. Most Mexican attacks have
occurred in the state of Veracruz.

The West Coast Attacks are rare
in the cold waters of the Pacific
Northwest, with just 20 attacks
reported from Canada to Oregon.
California leads all eastern Pacific
(US west coast) areas with 100
recorded attacks and an average

POSSIBLE CULPRIT
The silvertip shark is common in the
tropical Indo-Pacific, ranging to the coasts
of Central America. It has been known to
harass divers but has rarely been
positively identified as an attacker.

of three attacks per year since 1990.
The state's cool waters attract few
large inshore species and most
attacks have been credited to the
great white shark. Attacks occur
year round, but most have been
recorded from July to October.
Only 31 attacks have been recorded
between Mexico and Panama.

Attacking species Correct identification of many shark species is difficult even for trained scientists, so it is challenging to identify an attacking species from the often sketchy description given by a victim more intent on survival than taxonomic features. Nevertheless, based on more than 200 positive identifications, a number of species has been positively implicated. In Atlantic waters, the most frequently identified attackers, in descending order of frequency, are blacktips, hammerheads, bull and spinner sharks. Somewhat less frequently cited are sandbar, sand tiger, Caribbean reef, great white, lemon

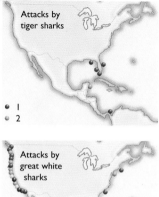

Attacks by tiger sharks

• 1
• 2

Attacks by great white sharks

• 1–3
• 4–6
• 7–9
• 10–28

GREAT WHITE ATTACKS
Although the great white attack rate along the Californian coast (as shown in the map above) remains steady, the number of divers meeting great whites underwater is increasing.

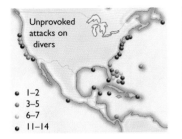

Unprovoked attacks on divers

- 1–2
- 3–5
- 6–7
- 11–14

Unprovoked attacks on surfers

- 1–3
- 4–8
- 44–72

Environmental factors Water temperature is an important factor in shark attacks, with 84 percent of attacks from the US Pacific coast reported from temperatures at or below 61° Fahrenheit (16°C). Waters here are cold and great white sharks, mainly cool-water dwellers, are responsible for attacks on humans that adapt to colder waters by wearing wet suits. Farther south in the Pacific, and throughout the Atlantic part of the region, attacking species are generally warm-water denizens that attack humans using the sea only during warmer seasons.

and tiger sharks. This listing probably accurately reflects the relative frequency of major attacking species, with the possible exception of the hammerheads. More than 90 percent of attacks from the northeast Pacific have been attributed to great white sharks.

The human factor When the region is looked at as a whole, attack victims are engaged about equally in three recreational activities: surfing (including rafting and kayaking), swimming (including wading) and diving (scuba and snorkeling).

There are, however, marked differences within the region. Divers on the Pacific coast are three times as likely to be attacked as those on the Atlantic coast. Conversely, swimmers on the Atlantic coast are twice as vulnerable to attack as those on the Pacific coast. Sharks do not discriminate between humans on the basis of sex or race. However, because aquatic recreation has historically been dominated by male Caucasians, 90 percent of recorded attacks in the region have been on males and 99 percent on Caucasians.

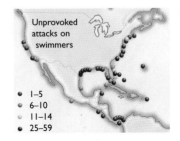

Unprovoked attacks on swimmers

- 1–5
- 6–10
- 11–14
- 25–59

245

ATTACK IN AUSTRALIA

Before the introduction of meshing on the eastern seaboard of Australia, the continent had the unenviable reputation of being the worst in the world for shark attacks. In recent years a number of fatal attacks off the Australian coasts have refueled the belief in sharks as savage killers. The facts, however, suggest otherwise.

SHARK SCAVENGER

The tiger shark is one of the few true shark scavengers and has consumed cattle, pigs, other animals and, indeed, humans that have fallen overboard from ships. Generally sluggish, it can move quickly when feeding.

Early records Rock carvings and paintings show that Australian Aborigines were familiar with several kinds of sharks. We will, of course, never know how many Aboriginal people were attacked by sharks while swimming or fishing. Early European settlers quickly became familiar with the sharks of Australian waters. One of the first recorded attacks occurred in Western Australia in 1803 when a sailor had parts of his clothing torn away by an attacking "monster." The first recorded fatal attack was in 1837, when a 12-year-old boy was taken in an east coast river.

Attack research It is surprising that, given the high incidence of attacks in Australian waters, no local full-time research is currently being undertaken on what provokes shark attacks. However, a comprehensive study was completed in 1958 by Dr. Victor Coppleson. Although now more than 40 years old, most of his findings still apply, although the interpretations he put on them are often now disputed. One of Coppleson's major discoveries was that most attacks occurred between two and six in the afternoon, and that the weather, tides and water clarity did not seem to be factors that influenced these attacks.

The rogue shark theory Coppleson's investigations confirmed that the majority of attacks in Australian waters were made by lone sharks and that only in a few

246

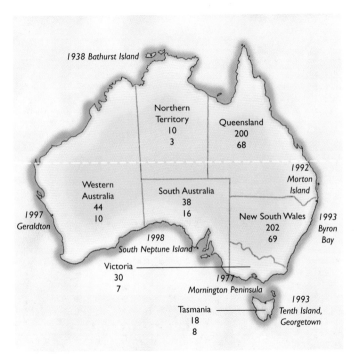

1938 Bathurst Island

Northern
Territory
10
3

Queensland
200
68

1992
Morton
Island

1997
Geraldton

Western
Australia
44
10

South Australia
38
16

New South Wales
202
69

1993
Byron
Bay

1998
South Neptune Island

Victoria
30
7

1977
Mornington Peninsula

Tasmania
18
8

1993
Tenth Island,
Georgetown

instances were shark packs involved. This led him to adopt what became known as his "rogue shark" theory. Coppleson found that places that had been free of attack for years would suddenly, within a short period and for no apparent reason, become the scene of multiple attacks. Then, just as suddenly as they began, the attacks would stop and the area would enjoy a long period free of attack. This pattern, he thought, was far too common to be a coincidence. Coppleson blamed individual or "rogue" sharks. This theory remains to be proven, and many experts are sceptical of it.

RECORDED SHARK ATTACKS

The map indicates the location of recorded shark attacks between 1791 and 1998. The top figure shown in each state or territory indicates the number of attacks that have been recorded there. The figure below indicates the number of recorded fatalities. The location and date of the most recent recorded attack in each state or territory is also noted.

ATTACK IN AUSTRALIA: Potentially Dangerous Sharks

Great white shark

Tiger shark

Great whites Great whites have accounted for 44 of the 168 cases in which the kind of attacking shark in Australian waters was identified. Despite its reputation, many cases have been reported of great whites inspecting divers without attacking.

Sevengill sharks One Australian attack has been attributed to a sevengill shark. These sharks are indiscriminate feeders of carrion and prey, but the recorded "attack" may have resulted from careless handling rather than a deliberate assault.

Wobbegongs Wobbegongs have been identified in 23 attacks, most of them probably provoked by careless fishers and divers.

Tiger shark Regarded as the most dangerous shark in tropical waters, the tiger shares with the great white and bull sharks membership of the "unholy trinity" of proven maneaters. It has been responsible for 30 known attacks in Australian waters. The tiger shark is one of the few species that actually consumes human prey—though it also has a reputation as a "trash can with fins."

Wobbegong

Sevengill shark

Hammerhead

Shortfin mako

Hammerheads Hammerheads have been implicated in only three recorded attacks in Australian waters. Of the nine species, only the great hammerhead is regarded as dangerous to humans.

Sand tiger The sand tiger, known locally as the gray nurse, has been identified in four of the recorded attacks in Australian waters.

Shortfin mako A common, active offshore and pelagic species, the shortfin mako is famed as a game fish. It has been identified in one attack in Australia. Its power, aggressiveness and sharp teeth make it a real danger to divers.

Blue shark The blue shark has been identified in only one attack in Australian waters. It is found around the world in temperate and tropical waters and grows to around 13 feet (4 m). The blue shark is a fast and aggressive predator.

Sand tiger

Blue shark

ATTACK IN AUSTRALIA: Statistics

Attack statistics Since records began in 1791, the Australian Shark Attack File has listed 542 attacks on humans in Australian waters. The records include both provoked and unprovoked attacks. Of these, 181 were fatalities—an average of one fatality per year. This average is being maintained: in the past 30 years, 31 recorded fatalities have occurred due to shark attack.

Length of Sharks Involved in Attacks

< 3 feet (1 m)	2%
3–6' (1–2 m)	23%
6–10' (2–3 m)	30%
10–13' (3–4 m)	24%
13–16' (4–5 m)	15%
>16 feet (5 m)	6%

The graphs, tables and diagrams on these pages summarize the records in the Australian Shark Attack File and provide an overview of the data that has been assembled.

Activity	Attacks	Fatal attacks
Swimming	83	45
Surfboard riding	40	4
Scuba diving	25	7
Hooka	1	1
Spearfishing	36	3
Snorkeling	15	3
Diving into water	1	1
Boat sinking	7	6
In shallow water	11	0
Fishing	13	0
Surf ski/sailboard & blow-up mattress	11	1
Feeding in captivity	6	0
Rescue of others	1	0
Waterskiing	1	1

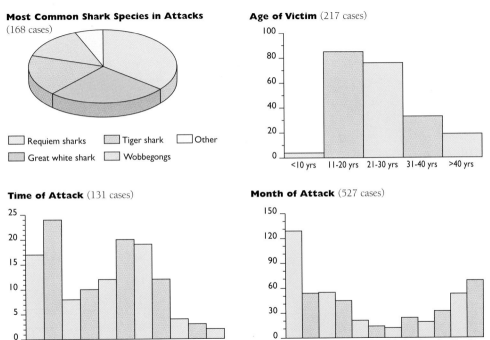

Most Common Shark Species in Attacks
(168 cases)

- Requiem sharks
- Great white shark
- Tiger shark
- Wobbegongs
- Other

Age of Victim (217 cases)

Time of Attack (131 cases)

Month of Attack (527 cases)

ATTACK IN SOUTH AFRICA

In the waters off South Africa there were 175 shark attacks between 1940 and 1990, which averaged about 3.4 per year and ranged from none to 10 per year. There were 35 fatal attacks over this period, averaging about 0.7 per year. In any one year, the range of fatalities was between none and four.

A variety of species The South African coastline, from the mouth of the Orange River in the eastern South Atlantic to the Mozambique border in the southwestern Indian Ocean, stretches for only 1,830 miles (2,950 km), yet includes in or near its boundaries (including Namibia and Mozambique) about 111 species of sharks. All eight of the orders occur here, and almost all of the families. There is every likelihood that additional species will continue to be added from incursions of tropical species and new discoveries. South African sharks are diverse, and include oceanic, continental shelf and continental slope species, wide-ranging circumtropical and circumtemperate sharks, local endemic species, cold temperate sharks, warm temperate sharks, and tropical–subtropical sharks

IDYLLIC BEACH
South Africa's many swimming and surfing beaches present an enticing scene but, like Australia, South Africa has an unenviable record for shark attacks. However, vigorous anti-shark measures, such as netting, in recent times have significantly reduced the risks to swimmers.

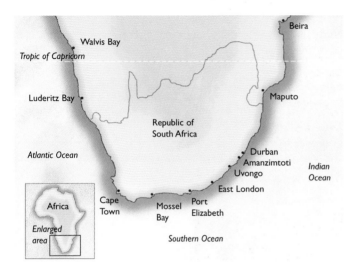

Where sharks attack The pattern of attack in South Africa may be correlated with temperature. No attacks on swimmers or divers have been recorded in the cold sector of the west coast of the Western and Northern Cape provinces from Cape Town to the Orange River mouth, though white sharks do occur there. In the Western and Eastern Cape provinces, between the Cape Peninsula and False Bay to off the Transkei coast, shark injuries on swimmers and divers have usually occurred at a low rate, although a recent (1998) flurry of attacks off the Eastern Cape is causing speculation. Between 1940 and 1990, 78 attacks occurred off the Cape provinces (about 1.5 per year), of which 10 were fatal. In the past few years several attacks have been reported in the Eastern Cape, including sand tigers biting bathers, and attacks by white sharks on surfers. Increasing shark incidents in these waters in postwar years are probably related to the growing popularity of water sports. The fatality rate is lower than kwaZulu-Natal and the principal species involved in Cape waters is the white shark. Some 97 attacks were reported in kwaZulu-Natal waters between 1940 and 1990, of which 25 (26 percent) were fatal.

ATTACK IN SOUTH AFRICA: Anti-shark Measures

OPPORTUNISTIC PREDATOR
One or two—and possibly more—injuries from shark attack in South African waters can probably be attributed to the tiger shark. This large, opportunistic predator eats a wide variety of prey, and is not averse to sampling unusual items. It rarely, however, acts aggressively toward divers.

The beginnings Protective measures against sharks were initially centered on the popular bathing beaches of Durban and south to Margate and Port Edward in southern kwaZulu-Natal. In 1907 the Durban City Council constructed a semicircular enclosure to protect bathers, which lasted 21 years before being demolished after corrosion and wave action had rendered it useless. For some years, the provision of protective measures lapsed.

The netting program Netting of Durban beaches began in 1952, following the success of a shark meshing program at Sydney beaches in Australia. Four other municipalities followed Durban in the early 1960s by installing anti-shark nets off their beaches. In 1964 local activities were centralized into what was initially titled the Natal Anti-Shark Measures Board but was renamed the Natal Sharks Board in the late 1980s. The Sharks Board is a kind of "shark police" that maintains the kwaZulu-Natal netting program and undertakes extensive research and public relations activities. It uses a fleet of skiboats, which are launched directly from the beaches or from nearby launch sites, to tend the nets. Six-man teams operate these boats and some 180 people set, retrieve, repair and rebuild the nets, which are set in a staggered double row offshore just beyond the surfline. The nets do not form an absolute barrier for the protected beaches and 35 percent of the sharks are caught on the landward side of the nets. At present, about 60 beaches are netted and more than 25 miles (40 km) of nets have been deployed along 200 miles (325 km) of coastline.

The future of netting The activities of the Sharks Board have generated controversy. Anglers, conservationists and some scientists are concerned about the ecological effects of long-term shark netting. In the 1980s some suggested that there seemed to be a marked increase in the number of juvenile sharks and attributed this to the shark nets. According to this view, which is not supported by Sharks Board researchers, the nets have depressed the number of larger sharks that feed in part on smaller sharks. However, this controversy was overshadowed in the late 1980s by the emotive conservation issue of catches of coastal dolphins in the nets and a possible decline in their numbers, and by concerns about shark conservation after the great white shark was protected in 1991. Although the catch of the shark nets is small compared to that of national commercial shark fisheries, with an average of about 1,400 sharks being taken each year for the past 18 years, anti-shark netting is an unselective and costly way of preventing small numbers of shark attacks. Alternatives and supplements are currently being tested.

POTENTIALLY DANGEROUS
The silvertip shark (below) is one of about 13 requiem sharks that are considered dangerous in South African waters. The great white (right), despite its reputation, rarely inflicts fatal injuries. Its approach is more likely to be inquisitive than aggressive.

ATTACK IN SOUTH AFRICA: Changing Attitudes

Sharks in context Although still widely feared by many, sharks are only minor contributors to human problems. In 1986 nearly 160,000 people died of all causes in South Africa, of which one was a shark fatality, while 166 were killed by lightning and nearly 1,300 by drowning. The maximum number of shark fatalities in any year has been four. However, the old anti-shark mentality is demonstrably, if gradually, changing, and many people now support shark conservation, including protection of the ultimate *Jaws* bogeyman, the great white shark, which South Africa pioneered in 1991.

Conservation and management The future of anti-shark measures in South Africa is uncertain, but as the public perception changes, evolving measures show signs of being transformed into policies analogous to those of game park management, where predators are regarded as positive assets. Sharks are increasingly viewed as assets that are more valuable alive than dead and as potent drawcards for expanding international tourism. Perhaps South Africa can become a place famed for its wide range of shark fauna.

Potentially dangerous sharks The table at right lists the 22 sharks that are considered potentially dangerous in South African waters. However, in South Africa, as in other countries, positive identification of sharks involved in attacks on humans is rare. It is possible therefore that some of the species listed have not in fact been involved in attacks.

TEMPORARY VISITOR
The blue shark is a long-distance traveler. It migrates regularly in the Atlantic, following the Gulf Stream to Europe, moves south along the African coast and then returns to the Caribbean.

Type	Family	Scientific name	Common name
sixgill and sevengill sharks	Hexanchidae	*Notorynchus cepedianus*	broadnose sevengill shark
nurse sharks	Ginglymostomatidae	*Nebrius ferrugineus*	tawny nurse
raggedtooth sharks	Odontaspididae	*Carcharias taurus*	sand tiger shark
mackerel sharks	Lamnidae	*Carcharodon carcharias* *Isurus oxyrinchus*	great white shark shortfin mako
weasel sharks	Hemigaleidae	*Hemipristis elongatus*	snaggletooth shark
requiem sharks	Carcharhinidae	*Carcharhinus albimarginatus* *Carcharhinus amboinensis* *Carcharhinus brachyurus* *Carcharhinus brevipinna* *Carcharhinus leucas* *Carcharhinus limbatus* *Carcharhinus longimanus* *Carcharhinus obscurus* *Carcharhinus wheeleri* *Galeocerdo cuvier* *Negaprion acutidens* *Prionace glauca* *Triaenodon obesus*	silvertip shark pigeye shark bronze whaler spinner shark bull shark blacktip shark oceanic whitetip shark dusky shark blacktail reef shark tiger shark sharptooth lemon shark blue shark whitetip reef shark
hammerhead sharks	Sphyrnidae	*Sphyrna lewini* *Sphyrna mokarran* *Sphyrna zygaena*	scalloped hammerhead great hammerhead smooth hammerhead

ATTACK IN NEW ZEALAND

Although shark sightings in New Zealand waters are fairly frequent and occasionally result in clearing of swimmers from the water and sometimes even scaremongering in the popular media, New Zealand beaches are generally safe places. Most sharks in the region are small, inoffensive and deepwater species.

Kinds of sharks There are more than 60 species of sharks in New Zealand waters. About 40 live in deep water and are encountered only by commercial fishers and scientists. Most of these are smallish, about 3 feet (1 m) or less in length, and, although they are clearly efficient predators, are not dangerous to humans unless handled carelessly when caught. A second group of six species is found in shallow coastal waters. Of these, the broadnose sevengill shark is the largest and most powerful and can be aggressive when caught. The third group

LOCATIONS
The map at right plots the locations of recorded fatal and non-fatal shark attacks in New Zealand waters. Despite the number of potentially dangerous species found around its coastline and the popularity of swimming and surfing, shark attacks are rare in New Zealand. The attacks recorded here are almost certainly incomplete. Many non-fatal attacks have not been reported to authorities or mentioned in the newspapers.

40°S

- Hauraki Gulf
- Auckland
- New Plymouth
- Napier
- Castlepoint
- Cape Foulwind
- Wellington
- Christchurch
- Oamaru
- Dunedin

• Fatal attacks
° Non-fatal attacks

comprises more than a dozen species of large, open-water pelagic sharks. Most range widely through the world's oceans, and many have been implicated in shark attacks. The great white and tiger sharks are the most dangerous, while the mako, blue shark and bronze whaler also pose a threat. Hammerheads are known for attacks elsewhere and must be treated with caution, while the porbeagle, though uncommon locally, is a potential danger.

Rare occurrences Despite the large number of people who use the water and the fact that potentially dangerous shark species are regularly in their vicinity, shark attacks in New

IN NORTHERN WATERS
Hammerheads are present around the North Island, particularly toward the north. They generally inhabit open coastal to offshore waters.

Zealand are extremely rare. There are too few to detect any common features. They are distributed right around the coastline with as many in the cooler and less populated south as in the north. Only a few of the sharks involved have been tentatively identified and suspicion generally falls on the great white shark. Three fatalities near Dunedin in 1964, 1967 and 1968 may have resulted from a single shark.

Humans at fault? In New Zealand, as in most parts of the world, conflict between humans and sharks is very one-sided. While there have been only 10 fatal attacks in more than 130 years a huge number of sharks have been killed by commercial and recreational fishers. Most shark species are slow-growing and long-lived with a low reproductive rate. They are thus highly vulnerable and are extremely susceptible to overfishing. Fortunately none of the sharks in New Zealand waters is endangered, but some numbers are declining.

The great white shark, though not common, has been blamed for attacks in New Zealand waters.

ATTACK IN THE PACIFIC

Any review of shark attack in the Pacific Ocean is burdened by at least three factors: the area's huge geographic expanse; the remoteness of many islands; and the lack or incompleteness of written records. In remote areas many shark attacks go unrecorded. Others may be noted only in local files.

Improving statistics Although shark attacks accounted for in the scientific literature probably represent only a small fraction of those that have occurred, the situation is now improving. As marine scientists and sports divers travel widely in the Pacific area and utilize now excellent communication networks, the proportion of attacks reported is probably higher than one might expect. With the revitalization of the Shark Attack File and the increasing use of the Internet, the likelihood of shark attack being reported has increased significantly.

LIVING WITH SHARKS

The indigenous people of the Pacific traditionally have an intimate relationship with the sea and interact with sharks regularly. They have therefore come to regard the danger of shark attack in a far more realistic way than do their continental counterparts.

FEEDING AND ATTACK

Attacks involving great white sharks in the Pacific, as elsewhere, are almost always related to feeding behavior. In the region, records of attack by this species are limited to Hawaii.

Interacting with sharks The indigenous people of the Pacific have a long cultural history that has been strongly influenced by the ocean and its living creatures. In most Pacific cultures sharks play central roles in religion, culture, fishing techniques and folklore, and may provide important resources for tools and weapons. Europeans, late arrivals to the Pacific, look on sharks very differently. It is not surprising therefore that an attack or incident in an area such as Hawaii will be reported more widely than one that occurs in an outlying island of the eastern Carolines. However, sports divers are increasingly seeking out opportunities to dive with sharks. Perhaps the outlook of seawise Europeans is approaching the traditional view of the cultures of the tropical Pacific.

A wartime accident Some attacks in the Pacific have clearly been the result of feeding behavior. The 1945 tragedy of the *USS Indianapolis* is an example. Four hundred sailors went under when the heavy cruiser was torpedoed; nearly 800 jumped clear and were adrift in the equatorial Pacific 187 miles (300 km) from the Philippines. During the next four days and five nights nearly 500 perished. It has been estimated that between 60 and 80 of them were killed by sharks.

Unlikely suspect While the tiny cookiecutter shark is not usually described as dangerous, it has been implicated in at least two recent attacks on humans in Hawaii. In 1992 the dead victim of a boating accident was recovered from the sea with two probable cookiecutter wounds. The non-fatal victim of an attack in 1995 was surfing in cloudy water off the island of Kauai.

SUSPECT SPECIES

The gray reef shark is one of 19 species that has been implicated in attacks on humans in the tropical Pacific. However, only in a minority of cases have attacking sharks been definitively identified.

TAKING PRECAUTIONS

Shark attacks have prompted various responses, ranging from fencing off, or netting, beaches to trying to eradicate the "problem." Some approaches focus on keeping sharks away from popular beaches; others aim to protect people in the water.

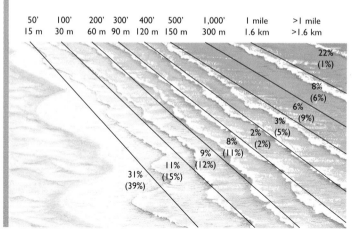

| 50' | 100' | 200' | 300' | 400' | 500' | 1,000' | 1 mile | >1 mile |
| 15 m | 30 m | 60 m | 90 m | 120 m | 150 m | 300 m | 1.6 km | >1.6 km |

22% (1%)

8% (6%)

6% (9%)

3% (5%)

2% (2%)

8% (11%)

9% (12%)

11% (15%)

31% (39%)

Protecting beaches In the past, attempts to keep people and sharks apart have included the use of barriers such as metal and wooden fences, electrical cables and even a wall of bubbles, emitted by a hose on the seabed. Expensive and difficult to maintain, none of these was widely used.

Netting programs Physically excluding sharks usually involves stretching long nets across the mouths of bays with swimming beaches. This is the method of

HOW FAR FROM SHORE?
The figures in the diagram, based on 570 incidents, provide a breakdown of attacks according to each victim's distance from shore. The figures in brackets show what percentage of people swim at these distances, indicating that attack statistics tell us nearly as much about the habits of people as they do about those of sharks.

choice in Australia and South Africa. However, netting is labor intensive; nets need regular repair, and often reinstallation after heavy storms; and sharks that become entangled in them must be removed. In both South Africa and Australia nets occasionally entrap other kinds of marine animals, including whales and dolphins. Recently, authorities in Queensland, Australia, have become involved in trials with acoustic signals to warn away baleen whales that are in danger of becoming entangled in shark nets.

Fishing programs Fishing programs to reduce shark numbers, in attempts to minimize the risk of shark attack, were used in Hawaii from the 1950s to the early 1970s. Such measures, however, are ecologically questionable, expensive and probably doomed to failure. Extermination of any species, especially a top predator, is inadvisable and probably impossible.

BEACH NETTING

Netting beaches on the east coast of Australia began in 1936 and 1,500 sharks were trapped from October 1937 to February 1939. In recent years up to 350 sharks a year have been caught, the most common of which are hammerheads. The illustrations show how nets are placed and secured. Each end of a 500-foot (150-m) net is secured by an anchor and its position is marked by floats, which also help to hold the net upright. The loosely hanging nets, about 20 feet (6 m) deep, are set by trawler in the late afternoon and usually hauled in the next morning. Not all beaches in the program are protected at any one time.

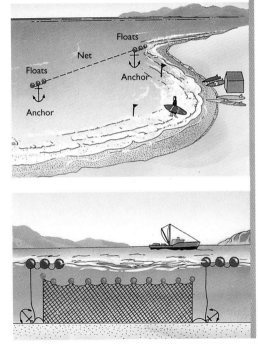

TAKING PRECAUTIONS: Repelling Sharks

Personal protection People have resorted to various methods to defend themselves from attacking sharks, including shouting at them, punching them on the snout and poking their eyes or gills. Although some undoubtedly survived, it is impossible to know how effective these methods are. Over the last half century, there has been an emphasis on deterrents that do not harm

ELECTRIC HARPOON
This paralyzes a shark by passing a large current at a low voltage through its body. Because of the cost of manufacture, it has not yet been produced commercially.

sharks. Designed to take advantage of sharks' keen senses, they have, however, had little success. For example, colored wetsuits resembling poisonous sea snakes were briefly investigated, but were abandoned when it was realized that sea snakes are part of the tiger shark's diet.

Chemical repellents A great deal of research has gone into chemical repellents. The United States Navy during World War II developed a product called Shark Chaser. The scientists involved knew that shark fishers believed—and indeed they still do—that sharks are repelled by the presence of decaying shark flesh. The repellent they created combined a chemical from decaying sharks with a black dye designed to spread out around the user to provide further protection by hiding them from the shark's view. A similar

SHARK POD
The battery-powered shark POD (Protective Oceanic Device) is the most effective deterrent yet devised.

compound—Pattern 1399—was devised by the British Admiralty. While Shark Chaser and Pattern 1399 undoubtedly provided comfort to those forced to use them, more recent tests have shown them to be of little value. Shark Chaser was abandoned in 1976. No search for a replacement has been started.

SHARK CHASER
Shark Chaser, a package of copper acetate and nigrosine dye, was issued to Allied personnel during World War II, but proved ineffective.

Shark POD One promising repellent, recently developed by the Natal Sharks Board in South Africa, is the POD (Protective Oceanic Device). This device attaches to a scuba tank and produces an electric field around a diver. When a shark encounters the field it is repelled and swims away. While initial results indicate that the POD is effective to a distance of about 23 feet (7 m), it remains to be seen whether it will be able to deter a large, highly motivated shark in feeding mode. As we learn more about sharks new ideas for repellents will undoubtedly be forthcoming. To date, though, the best advice to anyone floating in the water is to keep calm. Erratic movements may attract sharks.

TAKING PRECAUTIONS: Practical Guidelines

KNOW YOUR ENEMY
Left: Some sharks, such as the sand tiger, have been demonized for their size rather than for any aggressive disposition.
Right: Although they have unnecessarily killed many harmless sharks, powerheads, or bangsticks, can protect divers from potential threat from species such as these bronze whalers.

Shark cages Most shark cages are relatively lightweight and employed at or near the surface, where water movement is greatest. When diving in a cage, do not wear fins and keep at least one hand free. If the cage is jostled by an unexpected swell, or the ponderous bulk of a stimulated great white, you may need to stabilize yourself quickly to avoid being knocked about inside the cage. Such collisions can result in surprisingly painful, long-lasting bruises. Smaller, faster sharks—such as blues and makos—colliding with

a cage tend to ricochet off rather than slam it about. Since many dive operators attach baits directly to, or very near, the cage, take care that you remain entirely within its protective structure.

Spearfishing Remove speared fish from the water as quickly as possible, as their death throes often attract sharks. Reef sharks can move with astonishing swiftness, and deceptively slow-moving offshore sharks are often dangerously persistent. If you must retain your

INSIDE THE CAGE
The design of most shark cages is a compromise between protection for divers and opportunity for underwater photography. Sufficient space for cameras often means that a small shark can enter a cage and possibly injure a trapped diver. Most sharks that find their way into cages, however, are simply anxious to escape. In an emergency the cage can be winched to the surface.

catch underwater, do not attach speared fishes directly to your body; instead, use a long lanyard or stringer. If a shark contests ownership of a speared fish, prudence dictates unequivocal surrender of your catch. In its natural habitat, a shark has every advantage over a diver: speed, agility, striking range, exquisite senses and sharp teeth.

Underwater photography
Underwater photographers should be aware that their craft poses special risks. The optical properties of sea water demand close proximity to a shark to ensure crisp, clear images. This often causes inadvertent intrusion into the animal's kinosphere, or "personal space"— a roughly spherical region with a radius of about two body lengths that the shark may defend violently if persistently broached. The localized electromagnetic flux of a recharging strobe may elicit investigatory nipping or biting.

A THREATENED RESOURCE

Sharks are a valuable resource, but their harvesting must be carefully monitored and regulated if they are to be used and yet conserved. The harvesting of sharks for meat and other products predates recorded history, and every part of these creatures has been utilized by humans for some purpose. In recent times, however, their numbers have been dramatically depleted as a result mainly of modern industrial fishing techniques. Therefore the conservation of sharks—once thought to be the natural enemies of humans—is a matter of the utmost concern. National and international bodies are engaged in the quest for a sustainable policy that will ensure the survival of shark species.

USING SHARKS

Sharks provide a host of benefits. Their meat is eaten or used for fertilizer, and their fins are made into soup. Oil rich in Vitamin A is extracted from their livers, and anticoagulants from their blood. Their eyes provide corneas for transplants, and their cartilage has several medical applications. It is likely that a shark has provided meat for your table, lubricants for your machines, oil for your plants— even squalene for your cosmetics.

Sharks as food In the past, shark flesh was regarded by many Western consumers as inferior and even inedible, and was often marketed under alternative names, such as "rock salmon." Recently, however, shark meat (especially that of threshers and makos) has gained in popularity. Shark fin soup has been a Chinese delicacy for centuries, and the modern demand for shark fins has made them an extremely valuable commodity. Greek and Roman gourmets ate shark with enthusiasm, and it remains a staple of Mediterranean food as well as that of Asia and the Pacific.

HARVEST WITH CARE

While large sharks such as the sand tiger capture the public imagination, it is the smaller, less impressive sharks that sustain a global fishing industry and provide food for people throughout the world. Continued harvesting has put pressures on a number of species.

A VALUED RESOURCE

Virtually every part of a shark can be
utilized. The demand for shark products
is booming and nearly a million tons of
sharks are harvested by fisheries
worldwide. However, demand is beginning
to outstrip supply, and overfishing
threatens both the industry and the
sharks themselves.

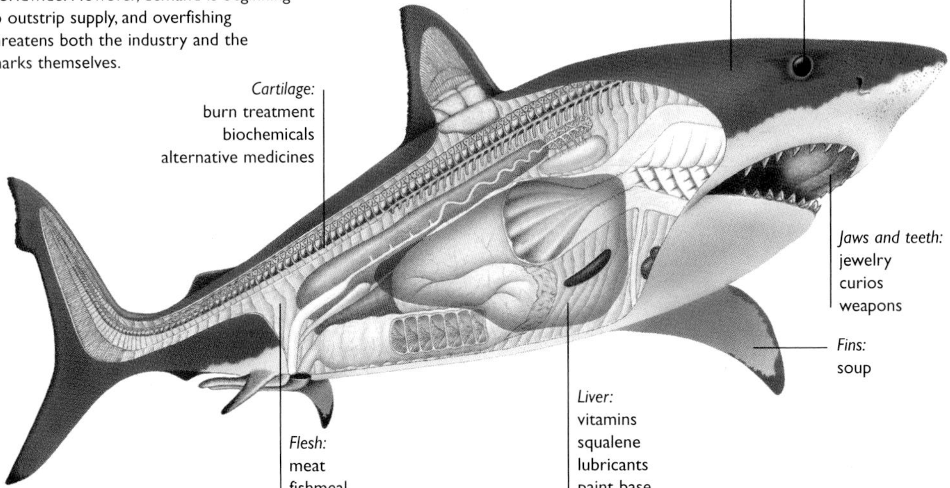

Skin:
shagreen
leather
abrasives

Eye:
cornea
transplants

Cartilage:
burn treatment
biochemicals
alternative medicines

Jaws and teeth:
jewelry
curios
weapons

Fins:
soup

Flesh:
meat
fishmeal
fertilizer

Liver:
vitamins
squalene
lubricants
paint base
cosmetics

USING SHARKS continued

Medicinal uses There is a growing interest in the medicinal uses of shark products. Shark liver oil has recently attracted interest for its pharmaceutical properties. Squalene, a compound found in the liver oil of deep-sea sharks, is used in medicines. Another property of shark liver oil, diacyl glycerol ether, is used in the treatment of wounds and burns and a substance derived from shark cartilage is used as artificial skin for burn victims. Recently, shark corneas have been used for human corneal transplants. There is an international industry producing powdered shark cartilage to meet the demands of users of alternative medicine for an anti-inflammatory agent for the treatment of arthritis and healing wounds after surgery.

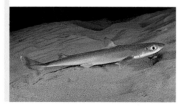

ICON AND RESOURCE
Above: A Pacific Islander displays an intricately carved shark model. Sharks have long provided inspiration for decorative crafts in the Pacific.
Left: The shortnose spurdog, a species of dogfish, is a valuable deepwater commercial species harvested from the southern oceans.

VALUABLE OIL
Shark liver oil, once prized as a lubricant and source of Vitamin A, has long been popular in Asia for its medicinal properties. It is becoming increasingly common in Western societies.

Artifacts from teeth Shark teeth have traditionally been used in many cultures for making functional, decorative and ceremonial objects. The Maoris of New Zealand used them to make weapons and ear ornaments. Inuit people made knives from them.

Using the skin The most characteristic feature of shark skin is its roughness, resulting from the placoid scales, or denticles, embedded in the skin itself. Historically, shark skin has been used as an abrasive and, in Asia, to decorate sword hilts and sheaths. Today, it is considered a food delicacy by many Asian cultures, and is used worldwide to make shoes, belts, handbags and wallets. Dried skin—called shagreen—was once used for polishing wood, although it has been supplanted by glasspaper or carborundum sheets. European artisans used treated shagreen for binding books and to cover personal artifacts. These articles are now valuable collector's items. It was not until World War I, however, that a way of tanning the skins of large sharks was found. The breakthrough was made when a chemical process that could remove the denticles without affecting the tanning process of the hides was developed.

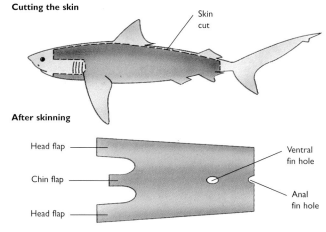

Cutting the skin

Skin cut

After skinning

Head flap

Chin flap

Head flap

Ventral fin hole

Anal fin hole

Final shape

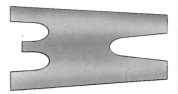

SKIN PRODUCTS
Dried but untanned skin, called shagreen, was once used like fine sandpaper for polishing wood. Boroso leather, made from the shagreen of small sharks by lightly polishing the scales to a high gloss, is an expensive specialty product. Shark leather has a higher tensile strength than leather made from cattle hides.

273

FISHING FOR SHARKS

For every human killed by a shark, 2 million sharks are killed by humans. Twelve million sharks are killed by humans each year, compared to six humans killed by sharks. At the rate at which shark fishing is proceeding, humans are jeopardizing world populations of apex predators that are essential to the health of marine communities.

How sharks are caught Sharks are captured using a variety of fishing methods, according to the species and its habitat. Coastal sharks are most often caught with gillnets set on the seabed, or with

longlines. Gillnets form an invisible barrier in which the shark is either gilled (caught by the head and gills) or entangled by the fins and body. Longlines consist of a main line with multiple branch lines, each of which ends in a baited hook. To catch open-ocean sharks longlines or gillnets are set close to the surface. Some small schooling sharks are captured by trawling giant mesh bags over the seabed to scoop them up. Huge basking and whale sharks are sometimes captured by small-scale traditional fisheries using harpoons.

HUNTER AND HUNTED
Above: Spearfishing is a popular Pacific sport. Although traditionally fish, including sharks, have been killed for food or as trophies, there is growing resistance to this form of recreational activity.
Left: This Galapagos shark has taken a baited hook and will trail the fishing line to the surface.

SUPPORTING AN INDUSTRY

Dogfishes are small to medium-sized sharks that are the basis of a global fishing industry, both for food and for other products derived from them. The piked dogfish, possibly the world's most abundant shark, is of particular commercial importance.

Modern fisheries Since the mid-1980s, demand for shark products has greatly increased. Many species of sharks have come under heavy harvesting pressure in North American waters. Historically, with a few regional exceptions, there have been few commercial shark fisheries in these waters. A significant harpoon fishery for whale sharks is now underway in the western Pacific. Scientists have plans to see whether the whale sharks of Ningaloo Reef, Western Australia, may travel to the area. It is estimated that the world trade of shark products exceeds USD240 million, although the real value is unknown because many markets do not reveal catch statistics

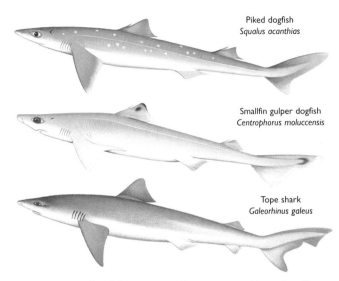

Piked dogfish
Squalus acanthias

Smallfin gulper dogfish
Centrophorus moluccensis

Tope shark
Galeorhinus galeus

Exploitation Modern fisheries continue to exploit a wide diversity of sharks, from small piked dogfish to large whale and basking sharks; from coastal to pelagic species; and from tropical to temperate seas.

There is strong evidence that all shark fisheries are over-exploiting their resources. Because of their small litter size and slow rate of reproduction, sharks are particularly vulnerable to overfishing..

THREATS TO SHARKS

In the past decade or so there has been a marked increase in the number of sharks harvested throughout the world. Fishing pressure is by far the greatest threat facing shark populations, and even if consumer demand for shark products suddenly declined, an unsustainable number of sharks would continue to be killed as bycatch.

ENTANGLED
A Port Jackson shark and an angelshark lie dead on the seabed after becoming entangled in a discarded fishing net in waters off the east coast of Australia.

Boom and bust In the face of unrelenting demand, there are few convincing examples of a sustainable shark fishery on a modern, commercial scale. Virtually every shark fishery that has been established has first boomed, then collapsed as a result of overfishing and poor management. This pattern can also be seen in traditional fisheries. In the Philippines in the late 1980s, for example, local people began fishing for whale sharks after traditional whaling operations had been halted. By the early 1990s whale shark numbers had declined. Prices soared as a result, putting increased pressure on the remaining depleted whale shark stocks.

Overfishing Despite overwhelming evidence of the consequences of overfishing, few management plans or restrictions have been implemented in any country or region. Sadly, for many species of sharks the best hope of long-term survival is that fishing becomes unprofitable before their numbers are reduced to unsustainable levels. As recently as the 1970s the United States Marine Fisheries Service was encouraging fishers to exploit sharks as an "underutilized resource." Largely as a result, shark

fisheries developed rapidly in the 1980s. Only in 1993, by which time shark populations off the Atlantic had declined by as much as 80 percent was a management plan finally implemented to reduce the fishing and finning of sharks and to allow shark populations to recover. Unfortunately, the same bleak

ACCIDENTAL VICTIMS

Right: The sand tiger shark's protected status in parts of the world has not protected this individual from falling prey to a baited hook.
Far right: This juvenile whale shark has survived an encounter with a fishing trawler but at the expense of its dorsal fin and the upper tip of its caudal fin.

GATHERING FOR THE HUNT

Divers on Heron Island, off eastern Australia's Queensland coast, gather with their equipment in preparation for a fishing expedition in the waters of the Great Barrier Reef.

scenario applies throughout most of the world. Of the 26 countries considered as major harvesters, only three—the United States, New Zealand and Australia—have implemented shark management plans.

Bycatch A serious threat to shark populations is that they are taken as bycatch by fishing operations that target other species. Blue and

thresher sharks, oceanic whitetips and other pelagic species are often caught on longlines set up to catch tuna and swordfishes. In 1993 it was estimated that 8.3 million sharks were caught by swordfish and tuna fisheries worldwide.

Other threats Shark control measures, such as the netting of beaches, have also put sharks under pressure. So too has the degree of human encroachment into shark habitats. A reason for this is that those habitats closest to areas of human concentration are among the most important to the viability of many shark populations.

CONSERVING SHARKS

There is today wide international recognition of the need to conserve sharks while exploiting them rationally, but this attitude is a recent one. Simply put, conserving sharks was not much of an issue before the early 1990s. Now, at least, scientists and conservationists are aware of the danger of extinction that some species face.

Sustainable fishing Only a small proportion of the shark population can be taken sustainably each year. The low natural mortality rate and well-developed young of sharks provide for remarkably stable populations. In a fishery where the

population size and the catch remain fairly constant over time, the population is in equilibrium and harvested sustainably. Here, there is a rough balance between the number of fish recruited to the population from reproduction each year, and the number dying from natural causes

TAGGING SHARKS
Tagging a great white shark. Researchers have developed ways to tag sharks with battery-powered transmitters that can record or transmit information about the tagged animal. Tags can relay data such as location, depth, compass heading and muscle temperature.

and from fishing. Fishing can be sustainable at many levels. Low levels result in small sustainable catches, and the population remains large. High levels can result in a similarly small sustainable catch, but the population becomes smaller, and the fishers have to work much harder to take the catch. The highest sustainable catches are obtained somewhere in between low and high levels of fishing. If the level of fishing is very high, so that total mortality is too high for recruitment to keep up, the population will continue to decline until it is either uneconomic to continue fishing, or the population collapses.

CAUGHT IN ERROR
This dead banded wobbegong was the victim of a bycatch. Millions of sharks a year are killed unintentionally by commercial or recreational fishers who are targeting other species.

Consumer education The most effective approach to shark conservation may come through consumer education. Although most people know that sharks are fishes, many still do not know that sharks' longevity and rates of reproduction differ from those of other fishes and that consequently sharks cannot be harvested in the same quantities. Since consumers are the ones who generate the demand for a product,

an educated consumer might decide that their need for shark products is not great enough to cause the demise of shark populations. Even the bycatch problem could be addressed by consumer boycotts, such as those targeted at driftnet fishing operations in response to the accidental killing of dolphins. We are presently witnessing a shift in the way people view sharks, from a sinister and expendable resource to a fascinating and ecologically vital inhabitant of our oceans. However, much work remains to be done, and it must be done quickly. It would be tragic if through carelessness and inaction we were responsible for the demise of creatures that have survived so many calamitous upheavals over the past 450 million years.

KEEPING WATCH
Keeping sharks in captivity is a controversial practice, but it does play a part in shark conservation by allowing scientists to study the habits and lifestyle of different species at close quarters.

CONSERVING SHARKS continued

Threatened species Several species of sharks that gather in coastal waters to feed or breed are regarded as vulnerable. Notably, large, maturing or mature great whites are easily caught when feeding around seal-breeding colonies. The decline in abundance of the great white has led to its protection in South Africa, Namibia, the Maldives, several states of the United States and Australia. The sand tiger is protected in New South Wales and Queensland in Australia. Dogfishes and chimaeras inhabiting

the continental slopes are taken as bycatch in several bottom-trawl fisheries. Much of the catch of these species is either discarded dead or not recorded. The dogfishes are likely to be particularly long-lived and to have relatively few young. Given the limited areas occupied by these species, and the intensity of fishing, some of the species of dogfish and chimaera are at risk of severe depletion in some regions. Some of the most threatened species are those occurring in freshwater habitats. These species are more vulnerable than those inhabiting marine waters, partly because the amount of fresh water in rivers and lakes is small compared with the amount of seawater on Earth. Moreover, tropical rivers and lakes where freshwater species occur are mostly in developing countries with large and expanding human

AMONG THE SHARKS
The observations and data collected by divers can be vital to the interests of shark conservation. The diver at left is examining a pair of juvenile Port Jackson sharks under the watchful eye of a blue wrasse. In the picture above a diver closely observes a zebra shark.

WELL UNDERSTOOD
The fact that both the crested bullhead shark (above) and the epaulette shark (right) cope reasonably well with aquarium life probably means that these are among the better understood species and that strategies for their conservation can be more easily devised.

populations. Such areas are much more vulnerable to exploitation than marine waters. Of particular concern is the Ganges shark, known from only a limited river system in the Indian subcontinent. Major international environmental groups such as the World Wildlife Fund are now turning their interest to the conservation of threatened sharks.

The way forward As sharks are being killed for so many reasons, there is no single solution to their decline in numbers. Governments need to develop and enforce a global response to shark management, perhaps in the same way the United Nations successfully banned the use of driftnets on the high seas. Other conservation measures may include developing techniques and fishing gear that reduce the numbers of sharks caught by fisheries targeting other fisheries. Unfortunately, any attempt to radically overhaul fishing methods would be likely to encounter stiff resistance from commercial operators.

Incomplete data Efforts to develop adequate management strategies for shark fishing are hampered by a lack of critical information about the basic biology, ecology and behavior of many species. Such information includes longevity, breeding patterns, migratory routes and location of nursery grounds. Clearly, much still needs to be learned.

A THREATENED SPECIES
Once feared and indiscriminately hunted, the sand tiger is one of a number of species now protected in some parts of the world. However, other species are not as fortunate.

A Threatened Resource

SHARKS IN CAPTIVITY

Sharks have been kept in captivity since the late 1800s and techniques for keeping them have improved greatly over the years. Not long ago, sharks were considered expendable. It was easier to replace a shark than to keep it alive, so they were caught, displayed, and then replaced when they died, with little regard for their well-being.

The situation today These days, great care is taken to monitor the health of sharks in captivity and to make sure they have an appropriate diet. At some aquariums sharks receive regular check-ups, including blood sampling and treatment for parasites and diseases. The construction and design of shark tanks have also come a long way in the last 15 years. Consideration is now given to the way in which sharks swim, with tanks being constructed in the shape of a figure-eight rather than a rectangle. Specially designed tanks are used to transport captured sharks by boat, truck and even plane.

IN THE WILD
While a small number of divers are privileged to view sharks in their natural habitat, such as here among coral reefs, most people observe sharks in the artificial environment of an aquarium.

SHARKS ON SHOW
Every shark kept in captivity represents a considerable financial investment, providing an incentive to aquariums to treat their sharks well and avoid having to replace them prematurely.

The case for captivity Sharks in the wild are difficult to observe. They range widely, may be dangerous, and live in a concealing medium. Therefore it is not surprising that much of our knowledge is based on studies of captive sharks at research laboratories or public aquariums. Just as importantly, displaying live sharks in aquariums gives people the opportunity to appreciate their beauty and grace in a simulation of

their natural environment. While many people do not have the time, money or inclination to dive with sharks in the open sea, most people have access to aquariums. Making sharks accessible to the community at large may be the key to changing perceptions of sharks and generating widespread public support for their conservation.

The case against captivity Those who object to sharks being kept in captivity claim that it is cruel to keep them in an unnatural environment and that confinement can affect their behavior, reproduction and, most importantly, their chance of survival.

There are limits to what extent we can extrapolate from studies of captive sharks to those in the wild. Reproductive studies, in particular, do not accurately reflect the situation for wild sharks. As a result, data from captive sharks have limited application to fishery management plans. The captive environment is a tradeoff between doing a disservice to a specific animal and benefiting sharks as a whole.

HANDLE WITH CARE
While this captive sand tiger is gentle enough to be hand-fed by a diver, sharks are highly instinctive and can never be considered tame.

STUDYING SHARKS

Until the last few decades, most of what we learned about sharks was derived from the study of dead specimens. By dissecting dead sharks, scientists were able to determine their internal anatomy, the structure of their skeletons and sensory systems, their diet, their method of tooth replacement and their various reproductive strategies.

Early studies Some of the earliest studies of live sharks were funded by the United States Navy, which was concerned by the threats sharks posed to its personnel and equipment. This research focused on the sensory biology of sharks, with the ultimate goal being the development of an effective shark repellent. Much of this research was conducted in tanks or shallow pens near the shore, where the ability of sharks to see, smell, taste and detect electric fields was tested.

A shift in emphasis While early research was driven by the desire to protect humans from sharks, much of the research over the last 20 years has been inspired by the need to protect sharks from humans. As shark populations have declined, it has become important to learn more about their biology and patterns of migration so that their populations can be protected and fishing can proceed on a sustainable basis. Because sharks are large and their skin is thick and quick to heal, it is easy to fit them with transmitters and tags so they can be tracked and monitored. Consequently sharks

KNOW YOUR SHARK

Far left: Researchers measure the dorsal fin of a whale shark in order to build up an "identity kit" that will allow the individual shark to be positively identified in future encounters.

Left: Hydrophones are useful tools in measuring sounds underwater. They enable researchers to track individual sharks and follow their movements.

SCIENCE AND RESEARCH

Shark research, like all marine science, demands a great deal of field work. Right: A diver collects Port Jackson sharks for use in research studies. Center right: An archival tag and spear barbs on a map of the Ningaloo Reef in Western Australia, which supports an important population of whale sharks. Bottom right: A marine biologist with an electronic tracking shark tag.

have been at the forefront of both tagging and tracking technology, and procedures used on them have since been applied to other open-ocean fishes such as tuna. The limitation of tag-and-release experiments is that they tell us nothing about the shark's movements between the time it is tagged and when it is recaptured. To obtain more detailed information, transmitters have been placed on, or in, some sharks. These allow scientists to measure not only the shark's horizontal movements but also the depth and temperature at which it is located.

OBSERVING SHARKS

The growing fascination with sharks is reflected in the increasing number of people prepared to pay to dive with them in their natural environment. Such dives either involve sharks being attracted to a dive site with bait or take place in an area where sharks are known to gather in large numbers. Depending on the location, divers may see several species and between one and more than 100 sharks. Not only do shark dives thrill observers and generate income for local dive operators—they also help to alter the popular perception of sharks.

IN THE FIELD

Careful planning is essential to ensure that your encounters with sharks are safe, environmentally sound, exciting and memorable. The best preparation is to gather as much background information as possible and to be aware of the hazards your chosen trip may involve. A good dive-travel agency will help you plan your trip.

DIVING SCHOOL
Scuba diving is a sport that must be taken seriously. Skills must be mastered in a pool (above right) and practiced with an instructor in the field (below).

Be prepared Before you leave home, study reference books and field guides to help you learn more about both sharks and your destination. Dive-travel magazines and brochures are also useful, although it is always worth checking the accuracy of these with an expert. Another good source of information is the Internet. Many operators, dive-travel agencies and divers with experience of sightings communicate this way. Be aware, however, that some of the information you glean many not be accurate.

Dive-travel hazards It is worth checking if a "travel advisory" warning has been issued by your government before you leave home. Some of the most exciting sites are in tropical areas, where divers may be exposed to health hazards ranging from severe sunburn to gastric upsets and even malaria. Never ignore coral cuts, which can become severely infected. Learn to identify marine species that can cause painful stings. Dive conservatively—do not exceed the recommended dive times and follow standard safety procedures.

GOOD GEAR
Investing in quality equipment will heighten your enjoyment of snorkeling. Make an investment in lightweight modern flippers, mask and snorkel.

Exploiting natural aggregations

Some dive operators take clients to areas known for their shark populations. Off Cocos Island, for example, scalloped hammerheads school by the hundreds. In Rangiroa, Tahiti, schools of reef sharks swim in a channel, paying scant attention to divers. In locations such as these, divers can observe sharks in their natural habitat.

DIVE WITH RESPECT
Above: This diver is blatantly disobeying shark-diving practice by touching the side of the whale shark.
Right: Snorkeling is an excellent way to explore coral reefs and view reef sharks in some parts of the Pacific.

Attracting sharks with bait

Some dives involve sharks being offered bait suspended on a line, or being hand-fed by divers. If large sharks are present, cages will be used. There are safety issues. Feeding sharks can be highly excited and there is a concern that they will associate divers with food.

PHOTOGRAPHING SHARKS

Capturing sharks on film or video can be a thrilling and satisfying exercise for many dive travelers. Fortunately for both amateurs and professionals, recent advances in technology make it possible to record all the drama of shark encounters.

Choosing a camera A beginner might choose a disposable camera in a waterproof housing. These cameras are inexpensive and call for little technical knowledge. They can produce a good result, particularly in shallow, sunlit, tropical waters. More serious photographers prefer amphibious 35 mm cameras with interchangeable lenses, underwater strobe lighting, variable focus and exposure control. These allow a much wider range of photographic composition and can cope with low light levels and limited visibility. It is possible to combine a land camera with a waterproof camera housing.

FILMING WITH SAFETY
Protected by a steel cage, a diver is able to capture clear video footage of a great white shark in its natural habitat. Because of the density of water, it is necessary to film at close quarters.

GETTING CLOSE

Divers need to exercise great care whenever they make a close approach to any large shark. They must be careful never to "corner" a shark and always to leave space for the subject of their photo or video film to retreat if it wishes.

Practical advice A dive buddy willing to act as a rear guard can be valuable, especially when there are numerous sharks about. It may sometimes be necessary to extend the camera and upper body through the windows of a shark cage to obtain a good angle. In these circumstances, a vigilant companion can warn of approaching danger.

Video equipment Video cameras, or camcorders, are extremely user-friendly. They are effective in low light, fully automatic and simple to operate. They provide more than an hour of continuous recording and the results can be viewed almost at once. A compact model is the best choice and the most popular format is Video 8 or High 8. To ensure quality footage, the camera must be held steady. Keep the action in the center of the viewfinder and shoot in sequences of wide shots, medium shots and close-ups. Beware of air bubbles on the lens port and are conspicuous when the image is viewed.

WELL EQUIPPED

The divers above are well equipped for a photographic dive in a low-light area. Strobe units and cameras, securely mounted on brackets, provide maximum flexibility. The Nikonos camera below has been designed for underwater use.

A SHARK OBSERVER'S GUIDE

The following pages list 20 places where you may come face to face with a shark in its habitat. In some areas access to sharks may be fairly easily gained and little planning is required. In others, sharks may be difficult to locate, though they are known to exist there. They may, for example, gather in an area for only limited seasons.

Planning Some sharks are found in remote locations. To see the silvertip sharks in Papua New Guinea, for example, or the sharks in the Galapagos Islands, you may have to take a trip on a live-aboard dive boat to reach the area. To see the whale sharks at Ningaloo Reef in Western Australia, you will need to plan your trip between late March and May, which is when these sharks congregate. Careful planning is essential to ensure that your encounters with sharks are safe, environmentally sound, exciting and memorable. The best course of action is to relax and observe sharks without interacting with them.

LORD HOWE ISLAND
This tiny island is in the Tasman Sea northeast of Sydney, Australia. Its coral reefs have formed a beautiful shallow lagoon, home to Galapagos sharks.

Preparing for a shark-viewing expedition.

SHARK VIEWING SITES
1   San Diego, USA
2   Kona Coast, USA
3   Sea of Cortez, Mexico
4   Revillagigedo Islands, Mexico
5   Cocos Island, Costa Rica
6   The Bahamas
7   Galapagos Islands, Ecuador
8   Isle of Man, UK

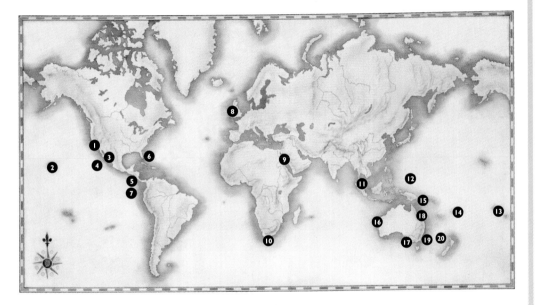

9   Ras Muhammad, Egypt
10 Cape Town, South Africa
11 Similan and Surin Islands, Thailand
12 Yap and Palau, Micronesia

13 Rangiroa Atoll, French Polynesia
14 Mamanuca Islands, Fiji
15 Valeries Reef, Papua New Guinea
16 Ningaloo Reef, Australia

17 Neptune Islands, Australia
18 Great Barrier Reef, Australia
19 New South Wales, Australia
20 Lord Howe Island, Australia

SHARK-VIEWING SITES

The challenge of observing sharks can take you from the Red Sea to the Galapagos via the Great Barrier Reef. These pages provide brief details about the top 20 sites: when to visit, likely weather, water temperature and possible hazards. They also list the diving amenities that are available and what kind of accommodation to expect.

San Diego, United States of America

When to visit Best diving conditions Apr–Sept
Weather Temperate year-round; summer mornings can be foggy, clearing by midday; rain and rough conditions most likely Dec–Feb
Water 59–70°F (15–21°C)
Dive logistics Cage diving with scuba gear from day boats or live-aboards for trips of three days; pre-booking essential; shore diving and snorkeling around kelp beds and rocky points
Accommodation A wide selection is available in San Diego, ranging from budget motels to bed and breakfast guesthouses and five-star resorts.

Kona Coast, Hawaii, United States of America

When to visit Fine year-round; humpback whale season Dec–May
Weather Warm days and cool nights; 70–85°F (21–29°C); gentle to brisk northeast trade winds; rainy Dec–Feb
Water 74–82°F (23–28°C)
Hazards Venomous animals include medusae and Portuguese man-of-war
Dive logistics Snorkeling from shore;

PAPUA NEW GUINEA
A local fishing canoe at Milne Bay in Papua New Guinea. Papua New Guinea is regarded as one of the top 10 dive locations in the world. As well as for its silvertip and other reef sharks, the region is famous for some very rare and bizarre marine species.

day boats and live-aboards for week-long trips (pre-booking essential) offer access to sites along the Coast
Accommodation A wide range, from beach camping and budget hotels to five-star resorts
Notes Bernice P. Bishop Museum, the archive of Hawaiian culture in Honolulu, has many artifacts relating to sharks. The University of Hawaii has conducted research on sharks for more than 50 years. Selected results are displayed at the University's Waikiki Aquarium in Honolulu,

RED SEA CORAL
Anthias dart about a coral reef in the Red Sea. Divers in the area commonly meet gray reef sharks searching for food.

along with a fine collection of living species. The aquarium is a comfortable place to see sharks.

Sea of Cortez, Mexico
When to visit Year-round; preferred diving season June–Dec
Weather Generally temperate to hot; 100°F (38°C) or more June–Sept; strong winds and tropical storms occur infrequently May–Oct
Water 70–80°F (21–27°C) June–Nov; 61–70°F (16–21°C) Dec–May
Hazards Variable weather conditions and occasional strong tidal currents
Dive logistics Day boats operate from La Paz and Cabo San Lucas; live-aboards offer 3–10 day excursions to Gulf Islands; pre-booking advised
Accommodation La Paz has a full range, from pensions, comfortable hotels, to high-rise luxury hotels.

Revillagigedo Islands, Mexico
When to visit Nov–May only, to avoid stormy Pacific waters and problems caused by offshore location

COURTING DANGER
Some dive operators attract and hand-feed sharks to entertain their clients. While there is an undoubted thrill in observing a shark close up, such activities change the shark's natural environment and are not to be encouraged.

Weather Tropically warm; often windy
Water 70–80°F (21–27°C)
Hazards Strong currents, rough water, and the remoteness of the location
Dive logistics Large, comfortable live-aboards only; book well in advance; boats depart from San Diego, USA, or Cabo San Lucas, which is closer
Accommodation Cabo San Lucas offers a range of accommodation from lodges to luxury hotels.

SHARK-VIEWING SITES continued

The Bahamas

When to visit Year-round; summer is hot, but the sea refreshes
Weather Influenced by trade winds; cooler Nov–Apr, warmest June–Sept; watch forecasts for tropical storms
Water 70–75°F (21–24°C) in Feb to 82–88°F (28–31°C) in Sept

CORAL WILDERNESS

In the tropical waters of Papua New Guinea divers are fortunate to observe not only sharks and other fishes but also spectacular corals and reef formations, such as the giant barrel sponge and gorgonian coral shown here.

Dive logistics Day trips from Grand Bahamas and New Providence; live-aboards also available; booking essential
Accommodation A wide range even on remote cays, from camping and comfortable dive lodges to luxury hotels; Walker Cay on Abaco Island has shoreside accommodation near Shark Rodeo.

Cocos Island, Costa Rica

When to visit Mar–Sept
Weather Cocos Island can be wet; offshore weather can be windy, with rough seas; trust the skipper to make a safe crossing and find the lee
Water Varies with currents; surface can be 80–82°F (27–28°C), with thermoclines much cooler
Hazards Strong currents and deep diving in a remote area
Dive logistics Live-aboards for 11-day trips, offering 7 full days of diving;

advance bookings with dive charter operators are necessary
Accommodation Large, comfortable live-aboard vessels are necessary because of the long ocean passage to Cocos Island; they accommodate between 12 and 22 divers
Notes This is a trip for avid and experienced divers only.

Galapagos Islands, Ecuador

When to visit Year-round, but best in late Feb–May
Weather Equatorial; warm to hot; cooler season from May–Dec; hotter season Jan–May
Water Variable with location and depth; from 65–80°F (18–27°C)
Hazards Blue-water diving with strong currents; this is not for novices
Dive logistics Live-aboards only; book packages through dive operators
Accommodation Live-aboards only, booking essential; hotels and

Isle of Man, United Kingdom

When to visit June to early Sept
Weather Cool, maritime climate
influenced by the warm Gulf Stream;
cool summers
Water 61°F (16°C)
Hazards Avoid becoming chilled
Dive logistics Day trips on local dive
boats and as volunteers with a well-
organized research project, the Isle of
Man Basking Shark Project; look up
its website at http://www.isle-of
man.com/interests/shark/index.htm
Accommodation Hotels and
guesthouses; special packages can be
pre-booked through travel agents
and dive operators.

VARIED SIGHTS

Far left: A New Zealand fur seal basks
on the rocky shoreline of one of the
Neptune Islands off the coast of southern
Australia. The abundance of these seals
and Australian sea lions attracts the area's
famous great white sharks.
Left: The zebra shark is widespread in the
tropical western Pacific and Indian oceans.

Ras Muhammad, Egypt

When to visit Best diving conditions
during warm months, June–Oct;
more variable visibility and risk of
rough seas during cool season,
Nov–Feb; sharks and manta rays
more in evidence during the mating
season, Dec–Feb
Weather Arid desert climate, hot
days, cooler at night; very little rain;
cool winds during Nov–Feb make
days cool and nights quite cold
Water 70–82°F (21–28°C)
Dive logistics Day boats, live-aboards
and shore-based diving from jeeps;
pre-booking recommended
Accommodation Excellent range, from
budget hotels to resorts.

guesthouses at Puerto Ayora,
Santa Cruz Island, but little or no
diving support
Notes Be aware of the political
climate in Ecuador which
can be unstable; check
government advisories.

SHARK-VIEWING SITES continued

Cape Town, South Africa

When to visit High season Feb–Sept, almost 100% likelihood of sightings; low season Oct–Jan, about 80% likelihood

Weather Usually pleasant, temperate; sometimes stormy and windy, or still and foggy

Water 58–65° F (14–18°C)

Dive logistics Day boats; day trips from Cape Town; overnight trips or 10-day excursions based at Gansbaai; book through dive operators

Accommodation A range of accommodation in Cape Town; guesthouses at Gansbaai, some self-catering

Notes During winter (June–Aug), high shark activity, but weather only permits trips to the island one or two days a week.

Similan and Surin Islands, Thailand

When to visit Best during the dry season, Nov–Apr; sunny, calm seas

Weather Tropical climate

Water 79–82° F (26–28°C)

Hazards Conditions are very wet during the monsoon season in Sept

Dive logistics Snorkeling or scuba diving from live-aboard boats for trips of 2–12 days; pre-booking recommended

Accommodation A wide range of resorts, hotels and guesthouses is available in Phuket.

Yap and Palau, Micronesia

When to visit Year-round

Weather Good year-round; trade winds May–Nov

Water 82–86°F (28–30°C)

Hazards Be extra alert when wreck diving; poisonous spiny trees on Palau, but only encountered if you hike inland to "jellyfish lakes" (highly recommended but no sharks)

Dive logistics Day boats and

MARINE WONDERS
A diver explores a Pacific coral garden. One of the great pleasures of diving is to see firsthand extraordinary sights that can only be imagined by non-divers. The Pacific is also the home of a number of reef and other sharks, and the enthusiast will find plenty to explore and observe.

live-aboards from all islands; a live-aboard amphibious airplane based at Palau visits outer islands, including Yap. Pre-booking before departure essential
Accommodation Palau has luxury hotels; Yap and Truk have comfortable hotels and lodge accommodation
Notes Yap offers best combination of indigenous culture and dive sites. Nitrox and rebreathers, and training in their use, are available on Yap and Truk.

Rangiroa Atoll, French Polynesia

When to visit Year-round, but best in Nov–Apr
Weather Excellent, although trade winds can blow strongly across low-lying atoll; sun protection is always necessary
Water Up to 80°F (27°C)
Dive logistics Day boats essential to dive the passes; pre-book through local Polynesian dive shops; also live-aboards
Accommodation Packages from Tahiti

by air include live-aboards or, more frequently, lodge-like shore accommodation; booking essential
Notes Strong currents make pass diving a challenge for beginning divers, and local guides expect some experience. Plan your trip carefully to permit ample diving between the infrequently scheduled flights.

VARIED HABITATS

Left: Tourists experience the thrill of diving with a whale shark at Ningaloo Reef off the coast of Western Australia. Below: A distinctive rock arch at Darwin Island, north of the Galapagos group. The region is famed for its shark fauna, including the Galapagos shark, collected here in 1904.

SHARK-VIEWING SITES continued

Mamanuca Islands, Fiji

When to visit Year-round; best weather in dry season (May–Oct)
Weather Daytime temperatures 68–86°F (20–30°C); mild, dry May–Oct; wetter, warmer Nov–Apr (wet season); highest rainfall and humidity in Jan–Feb; east–southwest trade wind
Water 83°F (28°C) from Nov–Apr; 80°F (26°C) May–Oct
Hazards Stonefish and medusae
Dive logistics Snorkeling and scuba diving from the shore, live-aboards or day boats; booking essential
Accommodation There is a full range of accommodation, from thatched fales to comfortable lodges and resorts; some resorts cater exclusively to the needs of divers
Notes Fiji is friendly and hospitable and has a rich culture. The region abounds with a variety of sharks, and the reef system for the most part has not been damaged.

Valeries Reef, Papua New Guinea

When to visit All year round
Weather Very warm, tropical; no distinct wet season

LORD HOWE ISLAND
A dive boat in the waters of Lord Howe Island in the Tasman Sea northeast of Sydney. This World Heritage Area is home to a number of endemic species and a rich marine fauna.

AN AUSTRALIAN GIANT
Jervis Bay, about 115 miles (180 km) south of Sydney, becomes the temporary home of thousands of Port Jackson sharks during the breeding season. It also shelters the world's largest cuttlefish species.

Water 79–82°F (26–28°C)
Hazards Malaria
Dive logistics Scuba diving from day boats or live-aboards; the snorkeling is excellent, but is not recommended where there are sharks
Accommodation Hotels in Kavieng; excellent live-aboards, booking essential
Notes Heed security advisories, particularly in the capital, Port Moresby. This is the most famous site in the world for silvertip sightings.

Ningaloo Reef, Australia
When to visit Late March to early May
Weather Warm, tropical, very sunny; afternoon sea breezes
Water 73–79°F (23–26°C)
Hazards Occasional cyclones
Dive logistics Snorkeling or scuba diving from day boats; some live-aboard boats, but not essential for good access
Accommodation Hotels, caravans and camp sites in Exmouth
Notes Avoid operators without spotter planes. Book your dive tours and accommodation before departure. Plan a minimum of five days' diving to guarantee many encounters.

GREAT BARRIER REEF
The Great Barrier Reef, off the northeast coast of Australia, is the only living thing that can be seen from space. At Scuba Zoo, at Flinders Reef in the Coral Sea, caged divers can interact with and photograph gray reef, whitetip reef and silvertip sharks.

SHARK-VIEWING SITES continued

Neptune Islands, Australia

When to visit Jan–May
Weather Temperate; very changeable from calm and hot to windy and cold; calm to quite rough seas
Water 61–66°F (16–19°C)
Hazards Seals can be aggressive when ashore; seek local advice
Dive logistics Cage diving with snorkel or scuba gear from live-aboard dive boats, trips from 3–16 days; pre-booking essential
Notes No guarantees; best shark sightings May–March.

Great Barrier Reef, Australia

When to visit Good conditions almost year-round; occasional strong winds; cyclone season late Dec–Apr
Weather Warm to very hot, tropical conditions; consistently dry, except during the cyclone, or wet, season
Water 72°F (22°C) in southern Queensland to 82°F (28°C) in northern Queensland
Hazards Venomous animals include the lionfish, stonefish, sea snakes, box jellyfish (or sea wasp), cone shell and blue-ring octopus. None is aggressive and accidents are rare, but learn to identify these species and their behavior
Dive logistics Day boats (be prepared for long trips to get out to the reef); live-aboards, trips of 4–8 nights mostly from Cairns and Townsville, pre-booking recommended as the area is a popular tourist site
Accommodation From camping to five-star resorts ashore or on coastal islands; also on several islands out on the reef; pre-booking recommended
Notes Shark feeding is not permitted inside the Marine Park.

New South Wales, Australia

When to visit Year-round
Weather Warm Oct–Mar, cool

MICRONESIAN MAJESTY
A giant clam is the focus of this Micronesian coral garden in the Pacific. Sharks and rays, an abundant tropical marine life, beautiful landforms, rich local culture and arguably the best wreck diving in the world make Micronesia a favored spot for divers.

Apr–Sept; no distinct rainy season
Water 57–70°F (14–21°C)
Hazards Rough seas during periods of strong offshore winds
Dive logistics Forster: day boats only; Jervis Bay: live-aboards or day boats, both offering equally good access
Accommodation Good hotels, guesthouses, camping and caravan sites at all locations
Notes An excellent region for self-driving, camping and exploring a diverse range of dive locations and sighting the plentiful marine species.

KEEPING WARM

Marine iguanas bask in the sun to raise their body temperatures before plunging into the water to feed. The Galapagos Islands are a nature lover's dream.

Lord Howe Island, Australia

When to visit Nov–May
Weather Cool, tropical summer, Oct–May; occasional unpredictable strong winds and regular rainfall; no distinct wet season
Water temperature 68–75°F (20–24°C)
Hazards The banded scalyfin, a very aggressive small fish, has a bite that can draw blood; swim away from its territory
Dive logistics Glass-bottom boats and day boats for snorkeling or scuba diving; pre-book during peak

SILVERTIP HAVEN

Diving in the tropical waters around Papua New Guinea.

season, Dec–Jan
Accommodation Small resorts and guesthouses, fully catered or self-catering; pre-book Dec–Jan
Notes Only 400 tourists are allowed on this World Heritage island at one time. It features a number of unique endemic land species as well as a rich marine fauna. Pack a waterproof coat for rainy spells and a warm jacket for cool evenings.

CLASSIFICATION TABLE

ORDER HEXANCHIFORMES
SIXGILL, SEVENGILL AND FRILLED SHARKS

Family Chlamydoselachidae—Frilled Sharks

Chlamydoselachus anguineus	Frilled shark

Family Hexanchidae—Sixgill and Sevengill Sharks

Heptranchias perlo	Sharpnose sevengill shark
Hexanchus griseus	Bluntnose sixgill shark
Hexanchus nakamurai	Bigeye sixgill shark
Notorynchus cepedianus	Broadnose or spotted sevengill shark

ORDER SQUALIFORMES
DOGFISH SHARKS

Family Echinorhinidae—Bramble Sharks

Echinorhinus brucus	Bramble shark
Echinorhinus cookei	Prickly shark

Family Squalidae—Dogfish Sharks

Cirrhigaleus asper	Roughskin spurdog
Cirrhigaleus barbifer	Mandarin dogfish
Squalus acanthias	Piked dogfish
Squalus blainvillei	Longnose spurdog
Squalus brevirostris	Japanese shortnose spurdog
Squalus cubensis	Cuban dogfish
Squalus japonicus	Japanese spurdog
Squalus megalops	Shortnose spurdog
Squalus melanurus	Blacktail spurdog
Squalus mitsukurii	Shortspine spurdog
Squalus rancureli	Cyrano spurdog

Family Centrophoridae—Gulper Dogfish

Centrophorus acus	Needle dogfish
Centrophorus atromarginatus	Blackfin gulper dogfish
Centrophorus granulosus	Gulper dogfish
Centrophorus harrissoni	Dumb gulper dogfish
Centrophorus isodon	Dark gulper dogfish
Centrophorus lusitanicus	Lowfin gulper dogfish
Centrophorus moluccensis	Smallfin gulper dogfish
Centrophorus niaukang	Taiwan or giant gulper dogfish
Centrophorus squamosus	Leafscale gulper dogfish
Centrophorus tesselatus	Mosaic gulper dogfish

Deania calcea	Birdbeak dogfish
Deania hystricosum	Rough longnose dogfish
Deania profundorum	Arrowhead dogfish
Deania quadrispinosum	Longsnout dogfish

Family Etmopteridae—Lanternsharks

Aculeola nigra	Hooktooth dogfish
Centroscyllium excelsum	Highfin dogfish
Centroscyllium fabricii	Black dogfish
Centroscyllium granulatum	Granular dogfish
Centroscyllium kamoharai	Bareskin dogfish
Centroscyllium nigrum	Combtooth dogfish
Centroscyllium ornatum	Ornate dogfish
Centroscyllium ritteri	Whitefin dogfish
Etmopterus baxteri	New Zealand lanternshark
Etmopterus bigelowi	Blurred smooth lanternshark
Etmopterus brachyurus	Shorttail lanternshark
Etmopterus bullisi	Lined lanternshark
Etmopterus carteri	Cylindrical lanternshark
Etmopterus compagnoi	Brown lanternshark
Etmopterus decacuspidatus	Combtooth lanternshark
Etmopterus gracilispinis	Broadband lanternshark
Etmopterus granulosus	Southern lanternshark
Etmopterus hillianus	Caribbean lanternshark
Etmopterus litvinovi	Smalleye lanternshark
Etmopterus lucifer	Blackbelly lanternshark
Etmopterus molleri	Slendertail lanternshark

Etmopterus perryi	Dwarf lanternshark
Etmopterus polli	African lanternshark
Etmopterus princeps	Great lanternshark
Etmopterus pusillus	Smooth lanternshark
Etmopterus pycnolepis	Densescale lanternshark
Etmopterus schultzi	Fringefin lanternshark
Etmopterus sentosus	Thorny lanternshark
Etmopterus spinax	Velvet belly
Etmopterus splendidus	Splendid lanternshark
Etmopterus tasmaniensis	Tasmanian lanternshark
Etmopterus unicolor	Brown lanternshark
Etmopterus villosus	Hawaiian lanternshark
Etmopterus virens	Green lanternshark
Miroscyllium sheikoi	Rasptooth dogfish
Trigonognathus kabeyai	Viper dogfish

Family Somniosidae—Sleeper Sharks

Centroscymnus coelolepis	Portuguese dogfish
Centroscymnus crepidater	Longnose velvet dogfish
Centroscymnus cryptacanthus	Shortnose velvet dogfish
Centroscymnus macracanthus	Largespine velvet dogfish
Centroscymnus owstoni	Roughskin velvet dogfish
Centroscymnus plunketi	Plunket shark
Scymnodalatias albicauda	Whitetail dogfish
Scymnodalatias garricki	Azores dogfish
Scymnodalatias oligodon	Sparsetooth dogfish
Scymnodalatias sherwoodi	Sherwood dogfish

Scymnodon ichiharai	Japanese velvet dogfish
Scymnodon ringens	Knifetooth dogfish
Scymnodon squamulosus	Velvet dogfish
Somniosus microcephalus	Greenland sleeper shark
Somniosus pacificus	Pacific sleeper shark
Somniosus rostratus	Little sleeper shark

Family Oxynotidae—Roughsharks

Oxynotus bruniensis	Prickly dogfish
Oxynotus caribbaeus	Caribbean roughshark
Oxynotus centrina	Angular roughshark
Oxynotus japonicus	Japanese roughshark
Oxynotus paradoxus	Sailfin roughshark

Family Dalatiidae—Kitefin Sharks

Dalatias licha	Kitefin shark
Euprotomicroides zantedeschia	Taillight shark
Euprotomicrus bispinatus	Pygmy shark
Heteroscymnoides marleyi	Longnose pygmy shark
Isistius brasiliensis	Cookiecutter or cigar shark

Isistius labialis	China Sea cookiecutter shark
Isistius plutodus	Largetooth cookiecutter shark
Mollisquama parini	Softskin dogfish
Squaliolus aliae	Smalleye pygmy shark
Squaliolus laticaudus	Spined pygmy shark

**ORDER PRISTIOPHORIFORMES
SAWSHARKS**

Family Pristiophoridae—Sawsharks

Pliotrema warreni	Sixgill sawshark
Pristiophorus cirratus	Longnose sawshark
Pristiophorus japonicus	Japanese sawshark
Pristiophorus nudipinnis	Shortnose sawshark
Pristiophorus schroederi	Bahamas sawshark

**ORDER SQUATINIFORMES
ANGELSHARKS**

Family Squatinidae—Angelsharks

Squatina aculeata	Sawback angelshark
Squatina africana	African angelshark

Squatina argentina	Argentine angelshark
Squatina australis	Australian angelshark
Squatina californica	Pacific angelshark
Squatina dumeril	Sand devil
Squatina formosa	Taiwan angelshark
Squatina guggenheim	Angular angelshark
Squatina japonica	Japanese angelshark
Squatina nebulosa	Clouded angelshark
Squatina occulta	Hidden angelshark
Squatina oculata	Smoothback angelshark
Squatina squatina	Angelshark
Squatina tergocellata	Ornate angelshark
Squatina tergocellatoides	Ocellated angelshark

ORDER HETERODONTIFORMES
BULLHEAD SHARKS

Family Heterodontidae—Bullhead Sharks

Heterodontus francisci	Hornshark
Heterodontus galeatus	Crested bullhead shark
Heterodontus japonicus	Japanese bullhead shark
Heterodontus mexicanus	Mexican hornshark
Heterodontus portusjacksoni	Port Jackson shark
Heterodontus quoyi	Galapagos bullhead shark
Heterodontus ramalheira	Whitespotted bullhead shark
Heterodontus zebra	Zebra bullhead shark

ORDER ORECTOLOBIFORMES
CARPETSHARKS

Family Parascylliidae—Collared Carpetsharks

Cirrhoscyllium expolitum	Barbelthroat carpetshark
Cirrhoscyllium formosanum	Taiwan saddled carpetshark
Cirrhoscyllium japonicum	Saddled carpetshark
Parascyllium collare	Collared carpetshark
Parascyllium ferrugineum	Rusty carpetshark
Parascyllium variolatum	Necklace carpetshark

Family Brachaeluridae—Blind Sharks

| Brachaelurus waddi | Blind shark |
| Heteroscyllium colcloughi | Bluegray carpetshark |

Family Orectolobidae—Wobbegongs

Eucrossorhinus dasypogon	Tasselled wobbegong
Orectolobus japonicus	Japanese wobbegong
Orectolobus maculatus	Spotted wobbegong
Orectolobus ornatus	Ornate wobbegong
Orectolobus wardi	Northern wobbegong
Sutorectus tentaculatus	Cobbler wobbegong

Family Hemiscylliidae—Longtailed Carpetsharks

Chiloscyllium arabicum	Arabian carpetshark
Chiloscyllium burmensis	Burmese bambooshark
Chiloscyllium griseum	Gray bambooshark

Chiloscyllium hasselti	Indonesian bambooshark
Chiloscyllium indicum	Slender bambooshark
Chiloscyllium plagiosum	Whitespotted bambooshark
Chiloscyllium punctatum	Brownbanded bambooshark
Hemiscyllium freycineti	Indonesian speckled carpetshark
Hemiscyllium hallstromi	Papuan epaulette shark
Hemiscyllium ocellatum	Epaulette shark
Hemiscyllium strahani	Hooded carpetshark
Hemiscyllium trispeculare	Speckled carpetshark

Family Ginglymostomatidae—Nurse Sharks

Pseudoginglymostoma brevicaudatum	Shorttail nurse shark
Ginglymostoma cirratum	Nurse shark
Nebrius ferrugineus	Tawny nurse or giant sleepy shark

Family Stegostomatidae—Zebra Sharks

Stegostoma fasciatum	Zebra shark

Family Rhincodontidae—Whale Sharks

Rhincodon typus	Whale shark

ORDER LAMNIFORMES
MACKEREL SHARKS

Family Odontaspididae—Sand Tiger Sharks

Carcharias taurus	Sand tiger, spotted raggedtooth or gray nurse shark
Carcharias tricuspidatus	Indian sand tiger
Odontaspis ferox	Smalltooth sand tiger or bumpytail raggedtooth
Odontaspis noronhai	Bigeye sand tiger

Family Pseudocarchariidae—Crocodile Sharks

Pseudocarcharias kamoharai	Crocodile shark

Family Mitsukurinidae—Goblin Sharks

Mitsukurina owstoni	Goblin shark

Family Megachasmidae—Megamouth Sharks

Megachasma pelagios	Megamouth shark

Family Alopiidae—Thresher Sharks

Alopias pelagicus	Pelagic thresher
Alopias superciliosus	Bigeye thresher
Alopias vulpinus	Thresher shark

Family Cetorhinidae—Basking Sharks

Cetorhinus maximus	Basking shark

Family Lamnidae—Mackerel Sharks

Carcharodon carcharias	Great white shark
Isurus oxyrinchus	Shortfin mako
Isurus paucus	Longfin mako
Lamna ditropis	Salmon shark
Lamna nasus	Porbeagle shark

ORDER CARCHARHINIFORMES
GROUND SHARKS

Family Scyliorhinidae—Catsharks

Apristurus acanutus	Flatnose catshark
Apristurus atlanticus	Atlantic ghost catshark
Apristurus brunneus	Brown catshark
Apristurus canutus	Hoary catshark
Apristurus fedorovi	Federovis catshark
Apristurus gibbosus	Humpback catshark
Apristurus herklotsi	Longfin catshark
Apristurus indicus	Smallbelly catshark
Apristurus investigatoris	Broadnose catshark
Apristurus japonicus	Japanese catshark
Apristurus kampae	Longnose catshark
Apristurus laurussoni	Iceland catshark
Apristurus longicephalus	Longhead catshark
Apristurus macrorhynchus	Flathead catshark
Apristurus macrostomus	Broadmouth catshark
Apristurus maderensis	Madeira catshark
Apristurus manis	Ghost catshark
Apristurus microps	Smalleye catshark
Apristurus micropterygeus	Smalldorsal catshark
Apristurus nasutus	Largenose catshark
Apristurus parvipinnis	Smallfin catshark
Apristurus pinguis	Fat catshark
Apristurus platyrhynchus	Spatulasnout catshark
Apristurus profundorum	Deepwater catshark
Apristurus riveri	Broadgill catshark
Apristurus saldanha	Saldanha catshark
Apristurus sibogae	Pale catshark
Apristurus sinensis	South China catshark
Apristurus spongiceps	Spongehead catshark
Apristurus stenseni	Panama ghost catshark
Apristurus verweyi	Borneo catshark
Asymbolus analis	Gray spotted catshark
Asymbolus vincenti	Gulf catshark
Atelomycterus fasciatus	Banded sand catshark
Atelomycterus macleayi	Australian marbled catshark
Atelomycterus marmoratus	Coral catshark
Aulohalaelurus kanakorum	New Caledonia catshark
Aulohalaelurus labiosus	Blackspotted catshark
Bythaelurus alcocki	Arabian catshark

Bythaelurus canescens	Dusky catshark
Bythaelurus clevai	Broadhead catshark
Bythaelurus dawsoni	New Zealand catshark
Bythaelurus hispidus	Bristly catshark
Bythaelurus immaculatus	Spotless catshark
Bythaelurus lutarius	Mud catshark
Cephaloscyllium fasciatum	Reticulated swellshark
Cephaloscyllium isabellum	Draughtsboard shark
Cephaloscyllium laticeps	Australian swellshark
Cephaloscyllium silasi	Indian swellshark
Cephaloscyllium sufflans	Balloon shark
Cephaloscyllium umbratile	Japanese swellshark
Cephaloscyllium ventriosum	Swellshark
Cephalurus cephalus	Lollipop catshark
Galeus arae	Roughtail catshark
Galeus atlanticus	Atlantic sawtail catshark
Galeus boardmani	Australian sawtail catshark
Galeus eastmani	Gecko catshark
Galeus gracilis	Slender sawtail catshark
Galeus longirostris	Longnose sawtail catshark
Galeus melastomus	Blackmouth catshark
Galeus murinus	Mouse catshark
Galeus nipponensis	Broadfin sawtail catshark
Galeus piperatus	Peppered catshark

Galeus polli	African sawtail catshark
Galeus sauteri	Blacktip sawtail catshark
Galeus schultzi	Dwarf sawtail catshark
Galeus springeri	Springer's catshark
Halaelurus boesemani	Speckled catshark
Halaelurus buergeri	Blackspotted catshark
Halaelurus lineatus	Lined catshark
Halaelurus natalensis	Tiger catshark
Halaelurus quagga	Quagga catshark
Haploblepharus edwardsii	Puffadder shyshark
Haploblepharus fuscus	Brown shyshark
Haploblepharus pictus	Dark shyshark
Holohalaelurus punctatus	African spotted catshark
Holohalaelurus regani	Izak catshark
Parmaturus campechiensis	Campeche catshark
Parmaturus macmillani	New Zealand filetail
Parmaturus melanobranchius	Blackgill catshark
Parmaturus pilosus	Salamander shark
Parmaturus xaniurus	Filetail catshark
Pentanchus profundicolus	Onefin catshark
Poroderma africanum	Striped catshark or pyjama shark
Poroderma pantherinum	Leopard catshark
Schroederichthys bivius	Narrowmouth catshark
Schroederichthys chilensis	Redspotted catshark

Schroederichthys maculatus	Narrowtail catshark
Schroederichthys tenuis	Slender catshark
Scyliorhinus besnardi	Polkadot catshark
Scyliorhinus boa	Boa catshark
Scyliorhinus canicula	Smallspotted catshark
Scyliorhinus capensis	Yellowspotted catshark
Scyliorhinus cervigoni	West African catshark
Scyliorhinus comoroensis	Comoro catshark
Scyliorhinus garmani	Brownspotted catshark
Scyliorhinus haeckelii	Freckled catshark
Scyliorhinus hesperius	Whitesaddled catshark
Scyliorhinus meadi	Blotched catshark
Scyliorhinus retifer	Chain catshark
Scyliorhinus stellaris	Nursehound
Scyliorhinus tokubee	Izu catshark
Scyliorhinus torazame	Cloudy catshark
Scyliorhinus torrei	Dwarf catshark

Family Proscylliidae—Finback Catsharks

Ctenacis fehlmanni	Harlequin catshark
Eridacnis barbouri	Cuban ribbontail catshark
Eridacnis radcliffei	Pygmy ribbontail catshark
Eridacnis sinuans	African ribbontail catshark
Proscyllium habereri	Graceful catshark

Family Pseudotriakidae—False Catsharks

| Gollum attenuatus | Slender smoothhound |
| Pseudotriakis microdon | False catshark |

Family Leptochariidae—Barbeled Houndsharks

| Leptocharias smithii | Barbeled houndshark |

Family Triakidae—Houndsharks

Furgaleus macki	Whiskery shark
Galeorhinus galeus	Tope shark, soupfin, school shark or vitamin shark
Gogolia filewoodi	Sailback houndshark
Hemitriakis abdita	Deepwater sicklefin houndshark
Hemitriakis japanica	Japanese topeshark
Hemitriakis falcata	Sicklefin houndshark
Hemitriakis leucoperiptera	Whitefin topeshark
Hypogaleus hyugaensis	Blacktip topeshark
Iago garricki	Longnose houndshark
Iago omanensis	Bigeye houndshark
Mustelus antarcticus	Gummy shark
Mustelus asterias	Starry smoothhound
Mustelus californicus	Gray smoothhound
Mustelus canis	Dusky smoothhound
Mustelus dorsalis	Sharpnose smoothhound
Mustelus fasciatus	Striped smoothhound
Mustelus griseus	Spotless smoothhound
Mustelus henlei	Brown smoothhound

Mustelus higmani	Smalleye smoothhound
Mustelus lenticulatus	Rig or spotted estuary smoothhound
Mustelus lunulatus	Sicklefin smoothhound
Mustelus manazo	Starspotted smoothhound
Mustelus mento	Speckled smoothhound
Mustelus minicanis	Dwarf smoothhound
Mustelus mosis	Arabian, hardnose or Moses smoothhound
Mustelus mustelus	Smoothhound
Mustelus norrisi	Narrowfin or Florida smoothhound
Mustelus palumbes	Whitespot smoothhound
Mustelus punctulatus	Blackspot smoothhound
Mustelus schmitti	Narrownose smoothhound
Mustelus sinusmexicanus	Gulf smoothhound
Mustelus whitneyi	Humpback smoothhound
Scylliogaleus quecketti	Flapnose houndshark
Triakis acutipinna	Sharpfin houndshark
Triakis maculata	Spotted houndshark
Triakis megalopterus	Spotted gully shark or sharptooth houndshark
Triakis scyllium	Banded houndshark
Triakis semifasciata	Leopard shark

Family Hemigaleidae—Weasel Sharks

Chaenogaleus macrostoma	Hooktooth shark
Hemigaleus microstoma	Sicklefin weasel shark
Hemipristis elongatus	Snaggletooth shark
Paragaleus leucolomatus	Whitetip weasel shark
Paragaleus pectoralis	Atlantic weasel shark
Paragaleus randalli	Slender weasel shark
Paragaleus tengi	Straighttooth weasel shark

Family Carcharhinidae—Requiem Sharks

Carcharhinus acronotus	Blacknose shark
Carcharhinus albimarginatus	Silvertip shark
Carcharhinus altimus	Bignose shark
Carcharhinus amblyrhynchoides	Graceful shark
Carcharhinus amblyrhynchos	Gray reef shark
Carcharhinus amboinensis	Pigeye or Java shark
Carcharhinus borneensis	Borneo shark
Carcharhinus brachyurus	Bronze whaler or copper shark
Carcharhinus brevipinna	Spinner shark
Carcharhinus cautus	Nervous shark
Carcharhinus dussumieri	Whitecheek shark
Carcharhinus falciformis	Silky shark
Carcharhinus fitzroyensis	Creek whaler
Carcharhinus galapagensis	Galapagos shark

Carcharhinus hemiodon	Pondicherry shark
Carcharhinus isodon	Finetooth shark
Carcharhinus leiodon	Smoothtooth blacktip
Carcharhinus leucas	Bull or Zambezi shark
Carcharhinus limbatus	Blacktip shark
Carcharhinus longimanus	Oceanic whitetip shark
Carcharhinus macloti	Hardnose shark
Carcharhinus melanopterus	Blacktip reef shark
Carcharhinus obscurus	Dusky shark
Carcharhinus perezi	Caribbean reef shark
Carcharhinus plumbeus	Sandbar shark
Carcharhinus porosus	Smalltail shark
Carcharhinus sealei	Blackspot shark
Carcharhinus signatus	Night shark
Carcharhinus sorrah	Spottail shark
Carcharhinus tilstoni	Australian blacktip shark
Carcharhinus wheeleri	Blacktail reef shark
Galeocerdo cuvier	Tiger shark
Glyphis gangeticus	Ganges shark
Glyphis glyphis	Speartooth shark
Isogomphodon oxyrhynchus	Daggernose shark
Lamiopsis temmincki	Broadfin shark
Loxodon macrorhinus	Sliteye shark
Nasolamia velox	Whitenose shark
Negaprion acutidens	Sharptooth lemon shark
Negaprion brevirostris	Lemon shark
Prionace glauca	Blue shark

Rhizoprionodon acutus	Milk shark
Rhizoprionodon lalandei	Brazilian sharpnose shark
Rhizoprionodon longurio	Pacific sharpnose shark
Rhizoprionodon oligolinx	Gray sharpnose shark
Rhizoprionodon porosus	Caribbean sharpnose shark
Rhizoprionodon taylori	Australian sharpnose shark
Rhizoprionodon terraenovae	Atlantic sharpnose shark
Scoliodon laticaudus	Spadenose shark
Triaenodon obesus	Whitetip reef shark

Family Sphyrnidae—Hammerhead Sharks

Eusphyra blochii	Winghead shark
Sphyrna corona	Mallethead shark
Sphyrna lewini	Scalloped hammerhead
Sphyrna media	Scoophead shark
Sphyrna mokarran	Great hammerhead
Sphyrna tiburo	Bonnethead shark
Sphyrna tudes	Smalleye hammerhead
Sphyrna zygaena	Smooth hammerhead

INDEX

Page references in *italics* indicate illustrations and photos.

INDEX continued

ACKNOWLEDGMENTS

TEXT The text for this publication has been drawn from research provided by George H. Burgess, Leonard J. V. Compagno, Carson Creagh, Kevin Deacon, Guido Dingerkus, Richard Ellis, Edward S. Hodgson, Kim Holland, Roland Hughes, C. Scott Johnson, Peter Last, John E. McCosker, Chadwick S. Macfie, John G. Maisey, Richard Martin, Arthur A. Myrberg Jr., A. M. Olsen, Larry J. Paul, Colin Simpfendorfer, Marty Snyderman, John D. Stevens, Leighton R. Taylor Jr., Valerie Taylor, Timothy C. Tricas, Terence I. Walker, John West.

PHOTOGRAPHS Kevin Deacon/Ocean Earth Images, Ron and Valerie Taylor.

ILLUSTRATIONS AND MAPS Martin Camm, Greg Campbell, Chris Forsey, Ray Grinaway, Gino Hasler, Frank Knight, Lorenzo Lucia, Kylie Mulquin, Tony Pyrzakowski, Roger Swainston, Steve Trevaskis, Genevieve Wallace, Rod Westblade.

CONSULTANT EDITOR Leighton R. Taylor is a Fellow of the California Academy of Sciences and a Research Associate of the Bishop Museum of the Waikiki Aquarium in Hawaii.